SEAN'S LEGACY

SEAN'S LEGACY
An AIDS Awakening

Robert Hopkins

TRIUMPH™ BOOKS
Liguori, Missouri

Published by Triumph™ Books
Liguori, Missouri
An Imprint of Liguori Publications

Library of Congress Cataloging-in-Publication Data

Hopkins, Robert, 1921-
    Sean's legacy : an AIDS awakening / Robert Hopkins. — 1st ed.
        p. cm.
    ISBN 0-89243-875-4
    1. Hopkins, Sean Patrick, 1964-1990. 2. Gay men—United States—Biography. 3. AIDS (Disease)—Patients—United States—Biography. 4. Gay men—United States—Family relationships. 5. Parents of gays—United States. 6. Homosexuality—United States—Religious aspects—Christiantity. I. Title.
HQ75.8.H66A3   1996
305.38'9664'092—dc20   95-41501

To my wife, Brenda, who brought Sean
into this world and joy into our lives

Acknowledgments

It was my friend Monsignor Robert Wister who first urged me to write this book, and I am particularly indebted to him for his encouragement, for his patience in proofreading my various drafts, for his guidance, and for his wise counsel.

I am grateful to Father Joseph Gallagher, a compassionate and sensitive man who has long ministered to people with AIDS, for his firm support, insights, and substantive assistance in the process of writing this book.

Dr. Keith G. Harkens, as a fourth-year medical student, generously gave me access to his medical books for reference. He also took time from his busy schedule to apprise me of the side effects of certain medications used to treat the Human Immunodeficiency Virus (HIV) and Acquired Immune Deficiency Syndrome (AIDS). His assistance saved me hours of independent research.

I thank Monsignor John Benson, our pastor, who knew Sean especially well, for providing me with the text of his homily at Sean's memorial service, and his personal recollections of our son. I also deeply appreciate his spiritual support during this long ordeal.

I am beholden to Dr. Anthony Fauci for his significant work at the National Institutes of Health, where he guides research in pursuit of an elusive vaccine and cure for AIDS, and for graciously reviewing portions of my draft to ensure its scientific accuracy.

Finally, I am most grateful for the assistance of Judy Keithline, who willingly and repeatedly rescued me from what I perceived to be computer disasters; and Jo Ann Hoggard, who typed the manuscript of this book with such speed and accuracy for presentation to the editor.

Remembrance

At the rising of the sun and its going down,
We remember them.

At the blowing of the wind and in the chill of winter,
We remember them.

At the opening of the buds and in the rebirth of spring,
We remember them.

At the shining of the sun and in the warmth of summer,
We remember them.

At the rustling of the leaves and in the beauty of autumn,
We remember them.

At the beginning of the year and at its end,
We remember them.

As long as we live, they too will live,
For they are now a part of us, as we remember them.

When we are weary and in need of strength,
We remember them.

When we are lost and sick of heart,
We remember them.

When we have joy we crave to share,
We remember them.

When we have decisions that are difficult to make,
We remember them.

When we have achievements that are based on theirs,
We remember them.

As long as we live, they too will live,
For they are now a part of us, as we remember them.
—From a Yom Kippur Memorial Service

Contents

Preface

Sean, our first and only child, died of AIDS on October 6, 1990, at the age of twenty-six. His memorial Mass was held in Our Lady of Victory Church, where he had served as sacristan. My wife, Brenda, sat by my side, and Don, Sean's devoted friend and companion, was next to her. We arrived early in that peaceful place to reflect undisturbed on Sean's life. The organ was playing softly.

In our church, there had never been any prayers for people with AIDS and those who cared for them, let alone acknowledgment that the AIDS crisis even existed. It was for this reason that we made it clear in his obituary that Sean was "gay" and had died of AIDS, a secret he asked us to keep while he was alive. We hoped that perhaps Sean's suffering and death from this terrible disease would bring about a change in the apparently unheeding attitude of our faith community.

Sean was concerned that he would be judged harshly by parishioners influenced by the unequivocal condemnation of homosexuality by the Roman Catholic Church. While the parishioners all knew and loved Sean, I feared that the Church's position would keep many of them away from this Mass. I was wrong.

The church began filling up. My sister, Diana, arrived with her two children. Dr. Stanley Talpers, our family physician, and his wife moved into our pew. He was the one who first discovered that Sean was infected with the Human Immunodeficiency Virus (HIV). Dr. Richard DiGioia, the AIDS specialist who cared for Sean during his long ordeal, was sitting across the aisle and I also saw Dr. David Bachman, Sean's compassionate ophthalmologist. Cathy Parrish, a wonderful nurse who so lovingly took care of Sean in our home, was nearby. Dorothy Goodman, the director of the Washington International School, which Sean attended, arrived along with several of Sean's teachers. As I looked around, I saw my associates from the Harry Hopkins Public Service Institute and many of our neighbors, former colleagues, and friends. The church was filled to capacity. It appeared that the entire parish community was present.

The organist started playing the hymn "The Church's One Foundation," and the procession advanced down the aisle. It was led by five altar servers, two of whom Sean had trained personally; six priests for whom Sean had served as acolyte at one time or another; and our pastor, Monsignor John Benson, who was wearing the Marian vestments we donated to the church. They all took their places, and the Mass began.

The familiar liturgy fell on my ears and had a lulling effect on me. Gradually, my sorrow-constricted heart relaxed. The organist played with great sensitivity, and the choir sang beautifully. Sean, who felt strongly that more Latin should be used in the Mass, would have approved of *Panis Angelicus* and *Ave Maria* sung in Latin in Teresa Foley's clear, pure voice.

I read the King James version of the Twenty-third Psalm because I preferred its beautiful imagery to the modern vernacular version decreed by Vatican II. Father Sara, one of the concelebrants, did the same at our request when he read the 121st Psalm.

In his homily, Monsignor Benson had this to say about Sean:

"Real disciples do not have and should not have a final fear of death. However, on an occasion like this, it does touch the deepest emotions. There will be a broken link in the chain of love in Sean's family. There will be special memories shared. As tears may cross the cheeks of those who loved him in this life, we know it is hard to hold back a measure of sadness, and we should not. Even Jesus cried when he learned of the death of Lazarus. In our hearts, our faith tells us that this is a victory celebration. One of God's faithful ones has gone home to Him. As Scripture tells us, 'All who seek the Lord shall dance for joy.' As we heard in the preface today, 'By death life is changed, not ended.' We can smile with tears that the Lord who conquered death has called Sean home to Him.

"Our grief is totally compatible with our faith, which never denies suffering, because suffering, in a mysterious way, is part of God's plan. Through suffering we can deepen our understanding of life. We know down deep in our hearts that Sean's death does not constitute the end of life, but the beginning of a new life. Our feelings of separation and grief are not to be feared or suppressed, for they are really symptoms of our love and our humanity. Together with the death and resurrection of Christ, we can gain new insights into this life and prepare for the glorious reunion in eternal life.

"Our sorrow and grieving are good, necessary, and human. Some years ago Sean became very interested in the Catholic Church. After much investigation and study, he was received into the Church together with

his mother and father. Sean's love of God and his
newfound faith was evident in the many hours of his
short life which were dedicated to God and his Church.
He touched the lives of so many with his compassion, his kindness, and his love. He was gentle, but
he held strong convictions. He was most knowledge-
able on many subjects and often served as an interpreter with our Spanish- and French-speaking people.

"We all experience life as a journey. Saint Augustine
put it succinctly when he said: 'Our hearts are rest-
less until they rest in you.' By our world's standards,
Sean's life was quite short. There were many things
left unsaid and many plans unfulfilled. We cannot
understand why, but can we fathom the mind of God?
It follows, therefore, that as life is a gift of God's
love, so our faith is a prerequisite of God's providence. We may not understand, but we must be confident that God's ways are good. Remember that
Sean, through all his suffering, never complained, but
now he is at peace with the God who made him,
loves him, sustained him, and has now called him
home. May he rest in peace! Amen."

The Mass ended with a thundering rendition of "A Mighty
Fortress Is Our God."

As we greeted those leaving the church, we were overwhelmed
by their outpouring of love for Sean and support for us. We
were deeply touched by the scores of sympathy letters and quan-
tities of flowers we received.

The realization that Sean died of AIDS brought home to our
fellow parishioners, probably for the first time, that this
terrible plague of AIDS was in our midst. That if Sean, some-

one they admired and loved, could die of AIDS, then so could others; and that they, as parents, might have to cope with the ordeal we had endured. This realization was, perhaps, the contribution Sean was destined to make to the community at large.

After the Mass, we invited Don and a group of Sean's other friends to our home, where we could comfort one another privately. These friends would become the nucleus of a much larger group of gay men, afflicted or threatened with AIDS, who would gather frequently at our home in the future.

There's so much good in the worst of us and so many faults in the best of us, that who am I—and who are you—to stand in judgment?

I

YEARS TO
REMEMBER

1

It was in London, in the spring of 1944, that Brenda and I first met. I was a twenty-two-year-old soldier, a combat cameraman with the U.S. Army Signal Corps, and Brenda was a breathtakingly beautiful English girl of eighteen with long dark hair and blue eyes.

I had returned to England to film the preparation for the Allied landings in Normandy after covering the landings and ensuing battles in North Africa and Italy. My younger brother, Stephen, a marine, had been killed just a month earlier in an invasion of the Marshall Islands in the Pacific.

Brenda had lived under the relentless bombing of London for the preceding four years. The train she took to school every day was frequently machine-gunned by Nazi aircraft. Her classes were interrupted by air raids, forcing her and her classmates into damp air-raid shelters where their studies continued to the accompaniment of the muffled thuds of bombs exploding above them. Too often one or more of her classmates did not show up at school because they had been killed or wounded by German bombs.

Brenda's father, an engineer, fashioned an air-raid shelter from an old steel fuel tank, which he buried in the back garden of their home. It was six feet long, five feet high, and four feet wide, with a vent for air and a small door at each end so they could escape from it if one door was blocked with rubble. It still smelled faintly of petroleum. There was barely enough room in it for Brenda, her mother, and her father. Here Brenda spent her nights during air raids.

By the time we met, we had both endured firsthand the trials and horrors of war. This created a bond and an understanding between us that has served us well through the years.

Our courtship flourished during that lovely spring. By then, Brenda was working in London close to my headquarters. We would lunch together whenever I was not out on assignment filming the consolidation of war materials and troops in preparation for the Normandy landings. Each evening we would go to the Red Cross club where we first met and spend the evening dancing and getting to know each other. On free weekends, we would ramble through Hempstead Heath or explore the ancient streets of London.

I proposed to Brenda in May, shortly after my twenty-third birthday, and she accepted. With some trepidation, I announced this fact to her parents. They were not enthusiastic, recognizing that their only child would be moving to America after the war.

Then I wrote to my parents, giving them the news, but mail delivery was unpredictable due to U-boat sinkings of our ships. It was not until I was in France that I heard from my mother. She thought I should wait until the end of the war before getting married. My father, on the other hand, said he expected to be in England soon and suggested we wait until he arrived so he could be at the wedding. But we were determined to get married as soon as possible. Brenda posted the marriage banns as soon as we were engaged, and a few days after Paris was liberated, I was able to get back to London briefly. We were married on August 30, 1944.

My subsequent assignments in Europe carried me through France, Belgium, Holland, Luxembourg—and into Germany as our armies advanced. We were 125 miles from Berlin when I was called back to Paris and assigned to cover the Yalta Conference. On my return from this assignment, I was awarded a field commission as a second lieutenant and assigned to London in command of a film unit there. Here I stayed with Brenda until the end of the war, filming, among my last assignments, the celebrations of VE-Day and VJ-Day.

After I was demobilized and Brenda and I were together in America, I worked in Hollywood as a screenwriter and in Paris with the Marshall Plan. We traveled throughout France while I wrote a guidebook. Later, for a number of years I was engaged in intelligence work that involved extensive travel in Europe. In the spring of 1963, the CIA transferred me to Argentina.

2

It was a sunny summer's day in Buenos Aires in November 1963. Brenda and I were relaxing on our terrace overlooking the broad Avenida 9 de Julio when we were startled out of our reverie by the sudden strident sound of a siren. It rose in pitch and then maintained a loud steady wail, more prolonged than the "all clear" signal in London after an air raid.

Puzzled, I thought at first there had been a short circuit in the electrical system controlling the siren. There was no one to ask about it, so I turned on the radio to try to learn the cause. All the stations intoned the same message: "President Kennedy has been assassinated." The siren was Argentina's way of announcing a catastrophe. We were shaken and stricken by the news.

During my thirty-five years of government service, I served in various capacities under eight presidents, from Franklin D. Roosevelt to Jimmy Carter. I knew several of them personally and felt a special affinity for two of them: President Roosevelt, who, because of my father's relationship with him, accepted me as a member of his unofficial family, and President John F. Kennedy, whose fresh approach to resolving national and world problems put a new spring in my step. I never met him, but I knew Arthur Schlesinger, Jr., who was closely associated with Kennedy. Arthur and I exchanged letters on U.S.-Argentine affairs throughout my three years in that country.

When President Kennedy was assassinated, Brenda and I mourned for his widow and children and for our nation. We felt that the United States itself was grievously wounded by this brutal and wanton act of murder.

A month after President Kennedy was killed, we learned that Brenda was pregnant. For us it was a miracle. We had ardently desired to conceive a child since our marriage in London in 1944. Now we began searching for a name for our unborn child, who, we were convinced, was a girl—though we had no medical evidence about the child's gender.

Under Argentinean law, all babies must be given a saint's name from the Catholic calendar. After reviewing these names, we selected Veronica Maria. The baby first kicked on Saint Patrick's Day, vigorous confirmation of her presence.

Born just weeks before our twentieth wedding anniversary, our child proved to be a boy. Since we were unprepared for this, the nurse handed Brenda a list of approved boys' names from the calendar. These included common names like "Juan" and "Pedro," in addition to unacceptable choices like "Modesto," "Narciso," and "Inocente."

In honor of President Kennedy, Brenda suggested we name our boy "John," but "John Hopkins" sounded too much like the university in Baltimore. Then Brenda, who is part Irish, suggested we call him "Sean," the Gaelic equivalent of John. Because he first kicked on Saint Patrick's Day, we added "Patrick" to his name. I had a hard time persuading Argentine officials to accept the name "Sean Patrick" when I attempted to register it, but they finally agreed because we were foreigners in their land.

The birth of Sean transformed our lives. When it seemed that we would remain childless, Brenda and I tried to give meaning to our lives in our work and our activities. But when Sean arrived, we focused all our attention and love on him. He was remarkably handsome, with blond hair and green eyes, and had a joyous demeanor. Argentines, most of whom had very dark complexions, hair, and eyes, stopped us in the street, marveling at the striking coloring and beauty of this child.

Unaccustomed to being around small children, we talked to Sean as we did to each other, so when he began to speak, there was no baby talk in his conversation. His mother spoke and sang to him in English, Spanish, Russian, and French so that his ear would become attuned to these languages at an early age.

When Sean was eighteen months old, we moved to Washington, D.C., bought a house, and settled there. On Mother's Day, 1969, I expressed my feelings about Sean and Brenda in a letter she has kept:

My Darling Brenda,

I have a vivid memory for that day in July in Buenos Aires—was it really only five years ago? The drive to the hospital, and the traffic ticket for that illegal turn (I was always a little miffed that I was never invited to explain this infraction to the judge). That idiotic receptionist at the hospital who would have had you stand around until the doctor arrived. Our chatter on inconsequential matters in your room to cover up our anticipation and anxiety.

Then you were taken to the delivery room and you were on your own. Alone and unable to do anything but wait, a terrible sense of frustration overwhelmed me. A thousand years later, the nurse came out carrying that red, bald baby boy—and the golden era of our life began.

Just look at him now. His strong, straight body, his tousled wheat-colored hair. His eyes, green or gray, or sometimes hazel, which flash with anger, sparkle with laughter, or melt with tenderness. And that voice of his, husky in the morning, earnest as he talks to his puppets, solemn as he casts a magic spell, and clear as he sings in his bath.

Most striking of all is his intellect, his imagination and his humor. At 4 1/2 years old, he is remarkable. Full grown, he can change the world and make it a better place.

This, and much more, is Sean—your creation. A product not only of your body but of your spirit. He is what he is because you are his mother, for which I thank God.

You are marvelous.

Robert

In due time, Sean went to preschool and kindergarten. His progress was well beyond his years; by the time he reached third grade, it was evident that our local public school was inadequate for such a precocious child. We enrolled Sean in the Washington International School (WIS), where he could develop his language skills and be exposed to a broad scholastic program.

Founded by members of the World Bank so their children could obtain a well-rounded education in keeping with their ethnic backgrounds, WIS also attracted the children of the international diplomatic corps in Washington. This gave Sean exposure to students from a variety of other countries. Learning a foreign language was a requirement, and Sean selected French. This meant that in addition to attending classes to learn that language, all of his other courses—mathematics, history, Latin, science, and geography—were taught to him in French.

Throughout Sean's childhood, we traveled frequently to Paris, where we had lived for many years before he was born. When our stay was a lengthy one, we enrolled Sean in a nearby school where foreign students were taught French. Most of the other students were Portuguese or Spanish, the sons and daughters of artisans and workers who had migrated to France. Sean was the only American. He felt awkward there at first; so to put him at ease, his teacher asked him to give a lesson in English to older students studying that language. From then on, Sean fit in and began to enjoy the school.

We lived in a small apartment we had bought in 1960, two years before leaving France for South America. It was built in the mid-seventeenth century as a private residence, then was divided into apartments after the French Revolution. In the process of restoring it, we uncovered the ancient hand-hewn beams in the ceiling and the original oak random-width plank floors.

Sean would help us with the ongoing restoration of the apartment and other odd jobs, for which we paid him. He spent the money he earned at the flea market. One of his prized purchases was a pair of Luna moths from Madagascar, which were box-framed under glass. (At this time, he was going through an intensive self-imposed study of butterflies and moths.)

The apartment was on the Rue Mazarine in the district of St.-Germain-des-Prés, just across the Seine from the Louvre Museum. Sean was enchanted by the Louvre, especially the Egyptian section, and we visited there often. He would take a small sketch pad and carefully draw the Egyptian inscriptions and wall paintings, oblivious to the museum visitors who formed a semicircle behind him, watching this solemn eight-year-old engrossed in his work.

Sean was intrigued by the mysterious civilization of Egypt and gave the study of it his full attention. He began collecting books on Egypt. He learned to identify the ancient Egyptian gods and the cartouches, or hieroglyph symbols of each of the pharaohs. Then, working with *Egyptian Language* by Sir A.E. Wallis Budge, in which ancient hieroglyphic texts were translated into English, Sean learned to read and write hieroglyphics himself. He thought it a remarkable coincidence that Jean-François Champollion, who was the first to decipher Egyptian hieroglyphics in the early nineteenth century, had lived only a few doors away from our apartment on the Rue Mazarine.

Left Bank antiquarians specializing in ancient Egyptian art welcomed Sean to their shops, fascinated that he knew so much about the pharaohs and their dynasties. He would spend hours with them discussing ancient Egypt. Often they would give him tomb beads or *shaouabtis*, mummy-shaped glazed-clay figures, usually blue or green, representing slaves of the pharaoh or dignitary buried in the tomb.

Brenda taught Sean to play chess, and he became adept at it. Soon I was no match for him. Once on the long flight across the Atlantic, Sean spotted a chess-playing couple and went over to watch. When they finished, he asked if he could play the winner. The man smiled indulgently. He accepted the challenge and lost the game to this small boy. Back home, Sean continued to play chess and formed a chess club at WIS.

Sean pursued all topics of interest to him with this same single-minded obsessiveness. I was envious of his ability to concentrate on a single subject to the exclusion of all others until he mastered it to his own satisfaction. By his own efforts, he broadened and deepened his knowledge. It was his decision to undertake the study of Mandarin as an after-school activity, despite the heavy load of his regular courses. Although two other students signed up for the course, both dropped out in frustration with the complexities of the language, leaving Sean with the benefit of studying with a private tutor. He enjoyed the language, the subtleties of pitch in speaking, and the graceful, brushed ideograms in writing.

He also studied calligraphy and, in his spare time, taught himself to write in various scripts, using calligraphy pens and colored inks. When we had dinner parties, he would write the names of guests on place cards in Gothic script.

Our son was popular with boys and girls alike. His quick

and sometimes biting wit caught his classmates unaware, convulsing them with laughter. At the same time, he had an almost courtly courtesy toward girls, who found him not only considerate and physically attractive but also an unusually interesting conversationalist. Unlike his classmates, who favored blue jeans and T-shirts, Sean had an innate flair for selecting casual clothes with a style that suited him.

Sean made much of the fact that he was born in Buenos Aires, a distant, exotic, and cosmopolitan city. When he returned from one of his several trips to Argentina to visit his godparents, he brought back a blue-and-white enameled plaque bearing the Argentine insignia, a miniature Argentine flag, and an Argentine shoulder patch, which he painstakingly stitched to the shoulder of one of his jackets. His friends often referred to him as "the Argentine," which pleased him enormously.

In all of his endeavors, Sean was a perfectionist. Winning was important to him, whether it was in tennis, swimming, or chess. When he lost, he was angry and impatient with himself. This impelled him to concentrate and practice until he excelled. This same perfectionism marked his approach to schoolwork and was reflected in his grades.

When Sean was still at WIS in 1981, Brenda and I discovered a house for sale in the Old Town section of Alexandria, Virginia, just across the Potomac River from Washington. It was a charming small frame house built in the late eighteenth century on one of the prettiest streets in Old Town Alexandria. It needed a great deal of work to restore it, but the price was reasonable, and the challenge intrigued us. We bought it with the intention of turning it over to Sean after we restored it so that he would have a home of his own when he graduated from college.

Brenda and I were proud of our son's accomplishments and felt certain that this remarkable child had come into our lives to make an important contribution to the world.

3

Sean's ethnic and religious heritage was diverse on both the maternal and paternal sides. Brenda was born in Lancashire in the North of England. Her father, Ben Stephenson, was swarthy and strong, and had the spontaneous sense of humor with which so many North Country men are blessed. During World War II, he worked long hours, frequently at night, building hydraulic pumps for the armed forces. When the German bombings of London became severe during the "blitz," Ben ordered Brenda to leave the city and evacuate to the relative safety of the countryside. He told her she must be gone by the time he returned from work. That evening when he opened the door, Brenda was still there. She refused to leave. In a rare display of emotion, with tears in his eyes, Ben took her in his arms.

Brenda's mother, Doris, was considered a great beauty in her day. She had blond hair, blue eyes, and a fair complexion. She often lamented Brenda's dark hair. A harsh disciplinarian, who was raised in the Ebenezer Baptist Church, Doris retained the austerity and severity of its concepts as part of her comportment throughout her long life. She died just before her ninety-ninth birthday.

Brenda remembers the days with her paternal grandparents as the happiest of her childhood. Her grandmother, Elizabeth-

Maria, was a Gypsy, but left the tribe at the age of sixteen when she married Ephraim Stephenson, a well-to-do magistrate twice her age. She bore him thirteen children, half of whom died in infancy or in early adolescence because of Elizabeth-Maria's mistrust of doctors.

Ephraim was an imposing man with a flowing white mustache. When Brenda knew him, he was virtually blind, and she would lead him by the hand. Yet he was an accomplished musician and often played the piano for her.

The Stephensons lived in a hillside house called Rose Cottage outside Burnley. Ephraim bought it for his young bride so that she could be near her sisters and the other members of the Gypsy tribe, who camped on the heights above her home during the winter months. Brenda remembers the house as having leaded-glass lattice windows and a swing in the garden.

Elizabeth-Maria maintained her contact with the Gypsy tribe. Taking Brenda with her, she frequently visited her two sisters and her friends in the Gypsy encampment.

Brenda remembers when she and her grandmother climbed up to the heights, crossing a farm and picking up apples from under the apple tree to feed to the Gypsy horses. When the irate farmer pursued them, Elizabeth-Maria gathered up the apples in her voluminous skirts, and they escaped by climbing over the farmer's fence. Gasping with laughter, they fled to the safety of the encampment. Here Brenda played with a little girl about her own age named Hazel, who had one blue eye and one brown eye. Together they fed the apples to the horses, then climbed into the Gypsy wagon that was Hazel's home, while Brenda's grandmother, smoking a clay pipe, gossiped with her sisters in the Romani language. Brenda still remembers some of the Romani words she learned as a child.

Her grandmother could neither read nor write, but she could read palms and Tarot cards. People came from far and near to have her tell their fortunes. In the tradition of all Gypsies, she had them first cross her palm with silver.

Elizabeth-Maria taught Brenda the lore of the Gypsies. She explained that Gypsies had to camp outside the city limits because they were prohibited by law from entering the city from sunset to sunrise. Anyone who violated the curfew was arrested, fined, and put in jail. Brenda now wonders if this was how her grandmother met the magistrate who became her husband.

In exchange for camping on private land, the Gypsies did odd jobs for the landowner. They were adept at training and trading horses, mending pots, weaving baskets, and telling fortunes. They were renowned for their music and dancing. In spring, they left their campgrounds and headed for seaside resorts throughout England, and even traveled to Europe. Here they applied their skills and talents and earned what money they had. Having little confidence in paper currency, they changed it for gold—which was good in any country. Brenda remembers her grandmother showing her a pouch that was secured with a cord around her waist under her many petticoats. In it were all her savings in gold sovereigns.

All his life, Brenda's father had an unfulfilled yearning to join the Gypsy caravan and travel with them as his brother had done. Although the general public feared the Gypsies, many people were intrigued by their apparent carefree way of life: Their births and deaths were not recorded; they had no identity papers; they did not serve in the armed forces; they paid no taxes; and their children did not go to school.

Local officials, however, persecuted the Gypsies and accused them of crimes they did not commit. The authorities tried to drive the Gypsies away by imposing curfews and forbidding them to draw water from public fountains, then labeling them as being unclean. The only protection the Gypsies had were their ferocious dogs. They trained the dogs to be fierce by placing their food where they could see and smell it but could not reach it. Brenda was warned to stay well away from them.

Whenever Brenda's grandmother baked pies, she always put one on the window sill so that a passing Gypsy or other needy person could help himself. She told Brenda that this pie was "for Albert," her brother who disappeared in Central Europe while traveling with the Gypsy tribe. She hoped that, wherever he was, someone like her would put a pie on a window sill for him.

Brenda's father often took Brenda to Blackpool Tower, a scaled-down version of the Eiffel Tower in Paris, to see the circus on the second landing. Here she enjoyed watching the elephants, lions, and tigers.

One morning, when she was five or six years old, Brenda told her grandmother that she had a terrible dream, so vivid, she was not sure it *was* a dream. In it, the Blackpool Tower had caught fire, and the wild animals were frantically trying to escape. A few days later, there was a front-page story in the newspaper that Hills Department Store in Blackpool, which was adjacent to Blackpool Tower, had caught fire and burned to the ground. A pet store on the top floor contained exotic young animals, all of which perished. In the photograph accompanying the newspaper article, the flames appeared to envelop Blackpool Tower.

Afterward, Brenda's grandmother, speaking in the familiar form used by all Lancastrians, solemnly told Brenda that she had "the gift." This gift, a kind of second sight, has manifested itself at various times in Brenda's life—including Sean's final hours.

Once, in the middle of the night, Brenda woke up and told me she heard her Auntie Ida, who lived in California, crying out to her, saying, "Help me, Brenda, help me!" So clear was this call that Brenda telephoned her aunt from Washington, but there was no answer. Brenda thought this strange, because her ailing aunt was homebound and had a twenty-four-hour nurse on duty. So Brenda called the local police in California and expressed her concern. They investigated and called back to report that her aunt had a stroke and was in the hospital.

On another occasion, when we were watching a television report of hundreds of people searching for a young boy who had disappeared from his home, Brenda suddenly said, "I can see him. He's lying facedown in a shallow stream. He's not moving." The next day, the searchers found the body of the boy exactly as Brenda had described it to me.

Brenda never considered these voices and visions a "gift," since they always related to illness or death.

With her parents, Brenda moved to London when she was eight years old. When she was ten, she and her family moved again, from central London to the western outskirts in Middlesex. Here she was irresistibly drawn to a beautiful small church near her home. Its precise age was unknown, but it was reputed to have been restored in the fourteenth century. Originally a Roman Catholic Church, it was taken over by the Crown after King Henry VIII severed ties with the Vatican and the Church of England was established.

Brenda began attending services regularly. Her Baptist mother disapproved, but Doris could not deflect her daughter's determination to adopt the Anglican Church as her source of spiritual support and enlightenment. Brenda was confirmed when she was twelve years old and eventually taught catechism to children of the parish. It was in this ancient church during World War II that Brenda and I were married.

~

My father, Harry L. Hopkins, was from Iowa, where his father, David, was a harness-maker, a dying trade in the early 1900s. This left David with plenty of spare time to pursue his favorite sport of bowling, to his wife's distress. My father's mother, Anna, was a pillar of the Methodist Church. She instilled in Harry a strong sense of responsibility toward the poor and underpriviledged. He moved to New York City after he graduated from Grinnell College in 1912, imbued with a commitment to enter a career in public service. He got a job as a social worker at Christadora House at five dollars a month plus room and board. He and my mother met there, fell in love, and were married in 1913.

My father soon proved his capabilities in the field of social services, and by the time he was twenty-five, he was director of the Southern Division of the American Red Cross, a job he held from 1917 to 1922.

Over the next decade, he took on increasingly responsible positions as assistant director of the Association for Improving the Condition of the Poor and then as director of the New York Tuberculosis and Health Association. In this capacity, he came to the attention of Franklin D. Roosevelt, then governor of New York. Governor Roosevelt appointed my father executive director of the New York State Temporary Emergency Relief Administration.

When Roosevelt was elected president in 1932, in the abyss of the Great Depression, he put my father in charge of the national work-relief program, which became known as the Works Progress Administration (WPA). In this colossal undertaking when most Americans were destitute, he put eight million of the unemployed to work building schools and libraries, repairing roads, and building highways. The WPA provided jobs to actors, musicians, writers, and engineers according to their skills. The fruits of their labors are still evident.

By this time, my father was a national figure, worshiped by most and vilified by some. He went on to become Secretary of Commerce.

In 1940, when it appeared that all of Europe would fall to the onslaught of the Nazi armed forces, President Roosevelt invited my father to move into the White House to work closely with him to develop national policy and strategy. My father was installed in the Lincoln Bedroom on the second floor and provided with a card table that served as his desk. Roosevelt appointed him his special emissary to Prime Minister Winston Churchill and later to Marshal Joseph Stalin to assess their military needs to combat Hitler. My father's assessments led to President Roosevelt's Lend-Lease Program to supply the British and the Russians with the weapons of war. The president then appointed him Lend-Lease administrator. He lived and worked in the Lincoln Bedroom for three-and-a-half years. (Until I went overseas with the army in 1942, I was a frequent guest at the White House and became well acquainted with the president and his family.)

My father retired from government service after President Roosevelt died. He was called back by President Truman, however, when the Russians began to undermine the formation of the United Nations at the San Francisco Conference. President Truman sent him to Moscow to deal directly with Stalin. In a series of frank, personal encounters with Stalin, my father resolved the problem, and the United Nations was saved. This was his last mission. He died at the age of fifty-five on January 29, 1946.

My mother and father were divorced after seventeen years of marriage. I was eight years old and hardly ever saw my father in the ensuing ten years. He remained, however, prominent in national affairs, and I avidly followed his career in *The New York Times*. To my mother fell the burden of raising my two brothers and me during the bleak years of the Depression.

My mother, Etelka, was born in Kaschau, Hungary, in 1886,

the eighth of ten children. Her parents were Orthodox Jews, and her father was a rabbi. He died when she was five years old. Three years later, her mother took her meager savings and migrated to America in steerage with her surviving children— my mother, my mother's sister, and my mother's two brothers.

Etelka was determined to put her Hungarian background behind her. She Americanized her name to Ethel and never spoke Hungarian to us, although she acknowledged to me when she was about sixty that she still understood it. When she and my father were married, she listed New York City as her place of birth. Unaware of this when I joined the army, I noted her true place of birth as Kaschau, Hungary. This caused a flurry of bureaucratic complications, which fortunately eventually dissipated.

After arduous study and avid reading, my mother lost all trace of her Hungarian accent. After school, she studied typing and shorthand and landed a job as secretary to Katherine MacKay, the wife of the wealthy Clarence MacKay, head of MacKay Telegraph. My mother traveled everywhere with Mrs. MacKay, including two trips to Paris, where they had a suite at the Ritz Hotel. My mother managed the household staff of seventeen at the huge MacKay estate on Long Island and helped care for their daughter, Ellen (who later became Mrs. Irving Berlin).

With Mrs. MacKay and other women's rights leaders, my mother became active in the women's suffrage movement. This opened her eyes to new challenges for her energies. She decided she wanted to do something else with her life, and asked Mrs. MacKay to release her. They parted on excellent terms, and Mrs. MacKay found her a job at Christadora House on New York's Lower East Side, working with impoverished children. She became attracted to Felix Adler's idea for improving the conditions of the poor, while stressing the secular basis for moral behavior. Breaking with family tradition, she joined Adler's Ethical Culture Movement, which she found to be more satisfying philosophically than the synagogue.

Also an active artist, my mother studied at the Art Students League in New York and with a Dutch painter in Woodstock, New York, who I knew only as "Schumaker." Later, when she moved to California, she studied under Hans Hoffmann.

My mother loved my father and always hoped he would return to her. It was only after he died that she remarried. When her second husband died, she moved to Australia to be near my older brother, David, and his family. She died there at the age of ninety.

4

When I was eight or nine years old and attending P.S. 166 in New York City, it seemed to me that religious wars were being fought on a daily basis on the school playground. When the Italian or Polish kids in my class asked if I were Catholic and I replied that I was not, they would gang up on me and beat me up. This prompted the Jewish boys to ask if I were a Jew. When I replied that I wasn't, they, too, beat me up.

In explaining my bruises to my mother, I said I didn't know to which church I belonged. "You must find one that conforms to your spiritual needs," she said.

It was not until 1932, when we moved out of the city to Westchester County, that I began to attend services in a variety of churches, searching for the "right" one. Although I searched diligently, I could not find one in which I felt comfortable. Some were too simple and spare, others too elaborate, with rituals I could not comprehend. This was particularly the case with the Roman Catholic Church. While I was uplifted by the organ music, the choir, and the beauty of the church, I could not understand the prayers in Latin and was puzzled by the responses of the parishioners. I was embarrassed and ill at ease at not knowing when to kneel, stand, or sit. Nor could I figure out what the priest was doing when his back was turned to the congregation. I decided that I could not find solace and strength in a church where I could not understand the liturgy.

To help me find my way, my mother enrolled me at the Mount Hermon School, a New England prep school founded by the Congregational evangelist Dwight L. Moody. Here Bible study was a required course, as was the study of comparative religions. I enjoyed these courses. I sang in the choir and took part in the annual Sacred Concerts. Still, I did not feel that this was the church I should adopt.

~

I've always felt close to God. I prayed to him frequently and sensed that he heard me. This was particularly true during World War II, when I was often in harm's way and felt his comforting presence.

Brenda, whose faith was always strong, was determined that Sean gain an understanding of Christian concepts at an early age. She taught him the Nicene Creed and the Hail Mary prayer. She also recited to him her favorite psalms, the 23d and 121st, which Sean learned by heart. I often think that the soothing words of these psalms gave him comfort and strength during the ordeal he later endured.

As he grew older, Sean was attracted to Our Lady of Victory Church, our nearby Catholic parish in Washington, D.C., much as his mother had been to the Anglican Church when she was a child. He sought more information and began to attend services. When he was thirteen years old, he told his mother he wanted to become a Catholic. She encouraged him to continue going to Mass, but urged him to wait for two years because this was such a serious, lifelong commitment. On the morning of his fifteenth birthday, he asked again. Brenda immediately called the parish priest and made arrangements for Sean to receive instruction. He always returned from these sessions full of enthusiasm.

Interested, I began to attend instruction with him, as did his mother. The pastor, a biblical scholar, conducted the instruction with patience and understanding. His clear explanations brought into focus the answers to puzzling questions. With some understanding of the mysteries of faith and the fact that the Roman Catholic Mass was now in English, I realized that at last I had found the church I had been seeking all my life.

At the Easter Vigil Service in 1980, I was baptized, and we were all confirmed in the Roman Catholic faith.

Sean trained and became an acolyte. He served at the daily Mass before school, as well as at all the Sunday Masses. Everyone in the parish came to know him. They were especially impressed by his reverence and devotion at Mass.

He was fascinated by the Church, its history, and the lives of the prophets and saints. He plunged into the study of Catholicism as he had studied Egyptology. He collected and read a large number of books on the subject, underlining passages of particular significance to him. When a new pastor, Monsignor John Benson, was assigned to our parish, he appointed Sean sacristan and put him in charge of training the other altar servers and assigning them to serve at the various Masses. Sean insisted they practice decorum appropriate to the occasion. Several parishioners expressed the hope to us that Sean would become a priest. Brenda and I were filled with pride when we attended services in which Sean took part.

One day after Mass, an elderly parishioner called Sean over to her car and commended him for the reverence with which he served at Mass. Then, with a wave of her hand, Rose Kennedy drove off.

In a recent conversation, Monsignor Benson recalled Sean as being "very kind, especially with the elderly, and with Spanish parishioners, for whom he gladly served as interpreter." We talked and reminisced about Sean's private battle with AIDS and, though Sean never discussed his being gay with the priest, Benson remarked that on occasion—especially when Sean would abstain from Holy Communion (while serving Mass)—he sensed an "inner" struggle.

"Sean was a living saint," Benson concluded, "who bore his cross bravely." The altar servers "idolized" him, and he never hesitated to volunteer his time—not only at church but at the rectory, where he was "a good secretary and typed well."

After Sean died, I discovered, among his books, prayers he had inscribed in English or Latin in gold-tooled leather-bound books with blank pages. He wrote these prayers in Gothic script, often illuminating them with gold and colored inks, creating his own personal breviary. Since these were obviously very important and meaningful to Sean, I've included a number throughout this book.

5

When Sean was a student at WIS, I thought it strange that we never met any of his classmates. We had installed a swimming pool in our garden, both for our own pleasure and to deal with Washington's torrid summers, and also for Sean and his friends. But Sean never invited his friends home. He said that his homework was so demanding that it took all of his spare time. And, indeed, the academic demands of the school did keep him occupied.

When he was about fifteen, one of his teachers told us that he had observed Sean after school in a café known to be frequented by gay men. The teacher said he thought we should be aware of this.

I went to the café myself and determined that while it may have been a gathering place for gay men, it had a lively mixed clientele of young people as well. When I mentioned his teacher's remark to Sean, he dismissed it, saying the teacher should mind his own business.

Sean was continuously besieged by telephone calls from girls, which tempered any concerns we might have had about his sexual orientation.

After he got his driver's license, I gave Sean my MG Midget so that he could drive himself to school, relieving his mother of this responsibility. Sean was delighted with this speedy little car and the greater degree of freedom it gave him. He immediately attached his Argentine plaque to the radiator grill and the miniature Argentine flag to the radio antenna.

Unfortunately, he had one accident after another, three of them so serious that the MG was virtually totaled each time. Although he was shaken, Sean was never really hurt. We managed to combine resources, and he gamely had the car rebuilt each time. But I began to worry. In fact, I had a foreboding that Sean would die prematurely. When I spoke of this to Brenda, she said she had exactly the same strong premonition. I felt that if Sean had another automobile accident, it would be fatal.

It was evident that the MG was a dangerous car. It was so small and close to the ground that drivers ahead of Sean could not see his car in their rearview mirror. Nor could Sean see around trucks or buses before attempting to pass them. So we decided that he should have a bigger and stronger car. We sold the MG and bought a Prelude for him.

A prerequisite for graduation from WIS was the successful completion of examinations for an International Baccalaureate (IB). Students who were awarded the IB qualified for acceptance in virtually any major university in the world. The examinations, including a thesis on a topic of one's choice, had to be written in the foreign language selected at the outset of studies and were judged by an independent panel in Geneva. Sean wrote a lengthy paper in French on the WPA American Guide Series produced by the Writers' Project during President Roosevelt's New Deal. He received an "A" on his thesis and his other IB exams and graduated as valedictorian of his class.

By this time, Sean had become interested in international affairs. He considered the possibility of joining the diplomatic service, and with this in mind, he applied to the School of Foreign Service at Georgetown University and was accepted in 1982. Sean decided to specialize in Latin American Studies and took up Spanish as a foreign language, which pleased me because I had been involved in Latin American affairs for many years until I retired in 1980.

Sean was stimulated by the exciting atmosphere of campus life and swiftly made new friends. Because our home was only a mile from campus, Sean continued to live with us. We fixed up our basement apartment for him. It had a separate entrance, which gave him a feeling of independence while keeping him close to us.

He received college credit for many of the courses in which he had excelled at WIS. This meant that he could elect to take courses of particular interest that he might otherwise have missed. He plunged into the college courses with his usual gusto.

But after Sean entered college, we began to notice disquieting signs. First, he announced that he was going to get a "butch" haircut. Stubborn though he was, we finally managed to talk him out of this. Then he began wearing a ring on his little finger that seemed out of character for him. Suddenly, it became evident that he was dyeing his already blond hair, turning it an awful orange hue. When I pointed out to him that people would think he was "queer," he just stared at me with his unwavering green eyes.

Sean became determined to get a deep tan. He not only sunbathed by the pool and on our boat, he spent an inordinate amount of time under a sunlamp in his apartment. One night, when we heard a strange moaning sound from there, we went down and saw Sean prone under the eerie greenish-purple light of the sunlamp with goggles over his eyes. He was wearing earphones with chrome bars that extended above his head, giving him a Martian appearance. The strange sound was Sean singing Gregorian chants in Latin in unison with a tape recording that he could hear, but we could not. It was an image we will probably never forget. We burst out laughing at the spectacle, which prompted Sean to sit up and remove his goggles. After a moment's confusion, he joined us in our laughter.

Still...some unexplainable anxiety filtered through me. And though I didn't try to understand it, there it was.

A SLIPPERY
SLOPE

6

$\int$ ean usually studied late at the university library, frequently returning home at one or two o'clock in the morning. He was conscientious in his studies, and he earned very good grades. But one night, to our consternation, he did not come home at all. We were frantic with worry. I went to the library and searched for him in vain. Then, at about six-thirty in the morning, he came through the door. Under our questioning, he said that he had worked late, then went out with a friend for relaxation and, since it was so late, stayed overnight. We pleaded with him never to stay out overnight without calling us. It was a promise he would not keep.

When, soon after, Sean began receiving telephone calls from men who identified themselves only by their first names, we decided it was time for a serious talk. We asked him point-blank if he was homosexual. He acknowledged that he was. But he refused to talk about it then, saying that we could discuss it when he returned from college that evening.

It was a quiet, sober discussion. In response to our question, Sean said that he knew he was "different" when he was eight or nine years old, although he could not define this difference from other children.

At the university, he said, he enjoyed being with girls and

dated them, but he was not physically attracted to them. He said he preferred the company of men.

In our discussion with him, Sean spoke frankly and answered all our questions candidly.

"I never chose to be homosexual. It's a natural condition. I have no control over it. I live with it, but I never would have chosen it. Do you really think I got down on my knees and prayed to God to make me homosexual? Why would anyone voluntarily expose himself to the stigma, the cruel abuse, and the derision of bigots and rednecks?

"Being gay means keeping that aspect of me secret from everyone outside the gay community. If it were inadvertently revealed, it could place my college career and job potential in jeopardy and sour my relations with the 'straight' world."

He acknowledged that dyeing his hair, wearing a ring on his little finger, and getting a dark tan were all silent signals to other gays that he was one of them.

"Most gay men feel constrained by society to remain in the closet," he went on. "Do you know that one man in ten is gay? Keep that in mind as you look at the men in our parish. Some even marry and have children to conceal the fact of their homosexuality. This, inevitably, leads to strained, unhappy marriages and often to separation or divorce.

"Some Catholic gay men have gone into the priesthood as their way of explaining to their doting parents why they don't get married. Some parents, convinced that their son has chosen a gay lifestyle just to defy them, banish him from their home and family. This cruel action against a child they had always nurtured and cherished will come back to haunt them, especially if he is stricken and dies of AIDS without their love and support.

"Suicide is not an unusual recourse for gays whose parents won't accept their condition or even discuss it with them.

"Gay men," Sean explained, "are everywhere, in every profession. They're doctors and lawyers, architects and engineers. They're factory workers and clerks, actors and artists, athletes and government workers, musicians and diplomats. They're Caucasians, African-Americans, Hispanics, and Orientals." He went on further, with a smile, "Interestingly enough, they are often handsome and usually highly intelligent, talented, and skilled, as if God were making up for the social burden they carry."

Then he said softly, "At least you won't have to baby-sit your grandchildren, because I'll never get married."

As Sean spoke, it was obvious that he was relieved that he could, at last, talk to us frankly about his homosexuality and that it was no longer bottled up inside him. His unburdening, though, lay like a weight on us. We had so much to think through, to worry about.

We cautioned him about AIDS and urged him to take proper precautions. He assured us he would, but I could see that he, like so many young people, thought he was invulnerable.

After Sean had returned to his studies, Brenda and I mused over his revelations. The term "confirmed bachelor" came to mind and took on an entirely new connotation for me in light of Sean's remarks. How often I had heard this term when I was young. Then, I thought it was a matter of free choice. Now, I know that it was a gay man speaking from the closet.

Early on, we assumed, as all parents do—and we especially since Sean was our only child—that one day after he completed his studies, he would get married and have children. In those early years, we devoted more attention to his well-being, his education, and his preparation for a career. It never crossed our minds that he was gay. Now our primary concern was for Sean's happiness, his future, and the grim possibility that he could be infected by the strange new fatal disease to which gay men appeared to be prone.

We had heard about "gay bashing," and we were concerned

about Sean's safety if word got out that he was gay. We had also heard about AIDS and gay promiscuity, which seemed to be as rampant in the early 1980s as was the sexual revolution of the 1960s. And, of course, we worried about his relationship with the Church, which viewed homosexuality with a baleful eye. Sean was truly devout, and his faith was an important element in his life. We decided that our responsibility continued to be to love, support, and protect our son. We continued to be haunted, however, by the premonition that Sean's life would be cut short. With this in mind, we decided that we would do all we could to make his life as rich in experience as possible.

I began to educate myself by reading any articles I could find describing AIDS. It was not an easy task. The medical terms were obscure, and diseases associated with AIDS were new to me and labeled with frightening-sounding names like "toxoplasmosis," "cytomegloviris," "pneumocystis pneumonia," "Kaposi's sarcoma," and "peripheral neuropathy."

I subscribed to an AIDS newsletter produced by the National Institutes of Health (NIH), which reported on various experimental protocols, but it was evident that no cure or vaccine for AIDS was in sight. This entry from Sean's handwritten book of prayers sums up our feelings at that time:

> *Lord, our God,*
> *you have sown in us your word*
> *Given us your son—he, who was beaten*
> *   and died for us,*
> *Is bread and life for the world,*
> *We ask you to let us find strength,*
> *to tread his path*
> *to let us be for each other.*
> *As fertile as seed and as nourishing as bread*
> *And thus lead a happy life.*

During Sean's college career, he dated one girl steadily, a beautiful Egyptian. Like Sean, she was a brilliant student and, intellectually, they had much in common. That they were constant companions concealed the fact to his peers that he actually preferred to be with men. This young lady really loved Sean, and her parents were fond of him as well, because he was respectful toward them and their daughter. Yet, in Sean's presence, they made it clear that as a Muslim, she could never marry a Christian and that if she did, she risked being stoned to death in Egypt. Sean assured them that he recognized this and that he regarded their daughter as a good and dear friend, nothing more.

This "relationship" provided Sean with a shield to fend off other coeds and avoid any insinuation that he might be gay.

In his junior year at Georgetown, Sean devoted even more time to his studies, but continued to see his friends in the gay community. He was constantly tired and began to lose weight.

By this time, Sean had a straight "A" average, and he spoke Spanish with native fluency. Hispanic members of our parish who spoke little or no English, would come to Sean to ask for advice or his prayers. They held him in high esteem and fervently encouraged him to become a priest.

If Sean perceived a contradiction between his homosexuality and being a devout Catholic, he never discussed it with us. (And we never brought it up, either.) I presume he considered this to be a matter between himself and his Creator: God created him as he was, leaving it to him to cope with this condition as best he could.

Because his studies were designed to qualify him for the diplomatic service, Sean thought that perhaps he could combine his passion for the Church with his knowledge of Latin American affairs. He toyed with the idea of studying for the priesthood after his graduation from Georgetown and set his sights on the possibility of serving the Church, after ordination, in the

Vatican Diplomatic Corps. But he soon abandoned this idea. "I can't change the way I am," he said, "even in the face of the Holy See's harsh condemnation of homosexuality."

This prayer composed by Father Joseph Gallagher reflects Sean's faith in God's providence, no matter what the struggle he endured:

> *Undying Father, boundless Ocean of Being:*
> *you are the God who was, the God who is, the*
> *God who is to come. Teach me to leave the*
> *past to your mercy, the present to Your love,*
> *the future to Your providence. Let me not*
> *look back in anger, nor forward in fear,*
> *but coax me gently to look around in*
> *constant, grateful awareness.*

7

On the morning of May 2, 1985, Sean did not feel well but went to the university anyway. When he returned at ten o'clock that night, he had a sore throat, chills, cramps in his legs and arms, and watering eyes. He had a fever of 103 degrees.

Our family physician diagnosed his condition as mononucleosis, which, he said, was common among students. He said there was no effective treatment other than to take aspirin every four hours and to drink plenty of liquids to avoid dehydration. According to our doctor, the illness could persist for three or four weeks.

Brenda called our pastor and told him Sean would not be able to work in the rectory or serve at Mass until he felt better. She also called our friend the Mother Superior at the Visitation Convent and others who knew Sean and told them of the serious nature of his illness. All said they would offer special prayers or Masses for his recovery.

Sean had to postpone one of his exams, but made it up later in the week. By the weekend, he was feeling well enough to resume his responsibilities at the rectory. Monsignor Benson had given him a salaried job there, substituting for the secretary during summer vacation. Combined with his job of training altar servers as well as serving at Masses on Saturdays and

Sundays, this meant Sean worked at the parish seven days a week.

In mid-June he suffered a relapse. The doctor diagnosed a form of hepatitis in addition to mononucleosis and ordered him to cut back to a five-day workweek.

Sean's condition improved by the time of the new school year, and he entered his senior year at Georgetown University's School of Foreign Service with the intention of pursuing the two-year graduate program for a degree in business administration. Tuition at the university had put a severe strain on our finances, and Sean recognized the importance of earning money during the summer to help pay for the master's program as well as to gain some practical experience in the world outside the confines of the university. Realizing, though, the need of additional funding, he applied for a private educational-aid grant. In support of his application, his professors submitted their high assessments of Sean's academic performance.

At the same time, Sean mailed a job application to the Central Intelligence Agency for an internship during the summer of 1986. He hoped that his performance at Georgetown School of Foreign Service and his Latin American studies would serve him in good stead with CIA personnel.

In early December, Sean was engrossed in studying for his final exams. He had no sooner completed these than he began a vigorous program of training the altar servers for the Christmas Masses at Our Lady of Victory Church. After Midnight Mass on Christmas Eve, at which all the acolytes served impeccably, we returned home and opened our Christmas presents. We retired at three-thirty in the morning and had to awaken Sean two-and-a-half hours later for his duties at the three Christmas Day Masses.

Sean's social life picked up after Christmas, and he attended parties almost every night, returning in the early (and sometimes late) hours of the morning. We never knew where he was or how we could reach him. We sometimes tried to reach his friends, but without success, and often spent agonizing hours at our front windows listening, waiting, for his car to come up our street.

On one occasion, we had a terrible argument with Sean about his irresponsible behavior. We told him about the anguish he was creating in us. He said nothing and left the house, slamming the door behind him.

Brenda and I went out, leaving a terse note for him saying we were shocked and hurt by his thoughtless behavior, and we had nothing more to say to him. After driving around for several hours, we finally confronted our worries. We could no longer cope with our fear for Sean's safety and the mounting aggravation his actions produced in us. Since Sean would soon be out of college, we decided that it was time for him to have a place of his own nearby. He declined our offer to move into the house in Alexandria, preferring to live in town, where he could be close to his friends and the Washington nightlife.

While he was in classes, we began to search for an apartment distant enough for him to feel independent but close enough for us to care for him should he need us. We found a handsome one-bedroom penthouse condominium apartment just a mile and a half from our home. It had a huge balcony overlooking the treetops of Northwest Washington. It was expensive, but we decided we could afford it. Sean was thrilled when he saw the apartment. We decided to buy it outright by mortgaging our home again, and to give it to him as a graduation present. The deed would be in his name as well as ours, and he would pay us rent sufficient to cover the monthly fees. Sean could hardly contain his excitement, but Brenda was saddened at the prospect of his leaving our home.

Soon afterward, Sean had a polygraph interview at the CIA

in connection with his application for a summer internship with that agency. He returned home very upset, angry and indignant. Following a four-hour interrogation, including questions he considered to be a gross invasion of his privacy, he was told he had to come back again for another session on the polygraph; but he told us he would never return to subject himself to that again and would never work for an agency that insisted on such an inquisition every three years.

Then Sean received a call from the Office of Educational Aid informing him he had won a three-thousand-dollar award for academic excellence. Sean was delighted but knew that he would still have to get a summer job as well to help cover his expenses.

Although his mononucleosis flared up again in the spring, Sean continued to study intensely, taking one final exam after another, for a total of five final examinations in May. Characteristically, he received an "A" on each of them—the end of a perfect senior year. At his graduation from Georgetown University on May 25, 1986, Sean received his Latin American Studies Certificate and was distinguished with the honor of graduating *cum laude*.

We were proud of his accomplishment and felt confident that he could step across the threshold from college to a career in international affairs, secure in the knowledge that he was intellectually prepared for the challenges it presented. After the ceremony, Sean returned home with us, and we celebrated his graduation and accomplishments with champagne. Then he went out with his girlfriend and other fellow graduates to celebrate with them.

When he returned, Sean declared, "That's it. My playacting is over. I'm no longer going to pretend I'm straight. Gays understand me, and I understand them." With this, he abruptly stopped going out with girls, including the Egyptian girlfriend he had dated for years. At the same time, he made it clear that he was not going to announce to the world that he was gay because bias against homosexuals was so strong.

Subsequently, Sean's girlfriend repeatedly telephoned Brenda to ask why Sean no longer called her. Obviously hurt and in tears, she plaintively asked what she had done to cause this. She said she and her whole family loved Sean and that her parents treated him as a member of the family. Brenda was sympathetic, but felt bound to honor Sean's wish not to be identified as a homosexual. Regretfully, she said she could not tell what the problem was. She urged Sean to speak to the girl himself, but he could not bring himself to do so.

8

Two days after Sean's graduation, his doctor called and asked if he could come to our home and see the three of us after dinner. At that time, he informed us that Sean's last blood test showed that he tested positive for the Human Immunodeficiency Virus (HIV). Sensing our concern, he quickly added that only 10 percent of those who test positive for HIV die of AIDS. (Such was the state of medical knowledge in May 1986.) He acknowledged that Sean was the first person he had encountered in his practice with HIV. Citing Sean's physically fit condition as a factor in his favor, the doctor cautioned Sean not to overtax himself with physical exercise, to eat well, and to get plenty of rest. Then he said he wanted to test Sean's blood every three months.

Sean was visibly stunned and subdued. It was as if his power, his strength, and his spirit had drained out of him. Later, he told Brenda and me he had already seen many of his friends become ill with and die of AIDS. Now he saw his own plans for the future grow dim.

When we talked to the doctor the following evening, he said, "The symptoms of mononucleosis are very similar to those of HIV, both being viruses. In view of this, very possibly Sean never had mononucleosis in the spring of 1985." He gave Sean the name of a specialist dealing with patients who were HIV positive and said he would send him the results of Sean's blood tests.

As the impact of this news sank in, Sean was devastated. Like so many young people, he never reflected that he might be stricken with a potentially deadly disease so early in life. Brenda and I were more realistic. While we were deeply distressed that our worst fears were coming to pass, we were not surprised. We had mentally braced ourselves for this.

Our thoughts were for our son. We held him in our arms and assured him that, come what may, we would always be at his side to take care of him. We had no concept of what lay ahead or what would be involved in caring for him. So little was known by the public at large about AIDS in 1986, and the material that I had been reading was designed more for medical researchers and doctors than for those of us who would have responsibility for daily care.

I drove Sean to almost all his doctor appointments, saw to it that he took his medications, and handled his health-insurance claims. This proved to be a daunting challenge as his health deteriorated and the number of his medications multiplied. The paperwork involved in his health-insurance claims was so confusing that I finally bought a computer to keep track of what had been paid and what we still owed.

I had to discipline myself to deal with these bewildering, yet necessary, details. I could not let myself forget for a moment which of the ever-changing medications Sean had to take and when. Here, again, I turned to the computer to record, adjust, and print weekly schedules of the medications Sean had to take at various intervals every day. It was fortunate that I was retired and had the time to devote to these tasks. Looking back, I must have seemed like a stoic while I tried to control my own emotions as Sean's condition worsened.

Brenda lavished on Sean her love, compassion, and full attention. She prepared special dishes for him, entertained him, and devised plans to divert his attention from his pain and anxiety.

I went with Sean to his appointment with the AIDS specialist on June 2. After examining Sean, the doctor told us that the average healthy man has a T4 blood-cell count of one thousand. "Sean's T4 count is over eight hundred," he said. "That's high enough to fight off AIDS-related diseases." Turning to Sean, he said, "This means that while you have the virus, you don't have AIDS. The HIV incubation period appears to be very long. During this period, only viral symptoms will be evident.

"HIV attacks and destroys T4 cells, which are responsible for fighting off disease," he explained. "When the T4 count diminishes to about two hundred, then the body's immune system can no longer fend off opportunistic infections. These infections then take over, and the patient is considered to have AIDS. This could take ten years from the time the virus infects the body; but, since you were not tested for the virus until the sixteenth of May of this year [1986], there is no way of knowing when you were actually infected.

"Even though you have no symptoms and might feel perfectly healthy," he warned, "you *are* infected and could pass that infection on to others with potentially fatal effects on them. For this reason, you must practice safe sex." Then he gave Sean a paper he had written on safe-sex practices.

We became better acquainted with this dedicated specialist in the next few years. Most of his patients seemed to be either HIV positive or afflicted with full-blown AIDS. He was laboring under the enormous shadow of treating AIDS, a disease for which there is still no cure. Angry as I was that the decline in Sean's health was irreversible, I had the greatest respect and compassion for the tenacity of this man who must have known in his heart that until a way is found to defeat this virus effectively, all his patients would die prematurely.

Before HIV appeared, the human immune system could fend off most diseases, including those that now take the lives of today's AIDS victims. But HIV attacked that immune system, weakening it to such a degree that the body was no longer protected. It was only a matter of time before the patient died.

In 1994, the Center for Disease Control (CDC) estimated that one million people in the United States were infected with HIV. But the magnitude of cases of HIV can only be guessed, because vast numbers of people who may suspect they are at risk refuse to be tested. They simply do not want to know that they are doomed to die in the near term.

Sean was able to move into his penthouse apartment on July 7. We took his bed from our house to his apartment and loaned him other pieces of furniture until he could buy furnishings of his own. It was an important step in Sean's life, and he relished the moment. He was eager to get on with this new phase of his career and was equally determined not to be deterred by the ominous news he had just received.

His health remained good throughout the summer. He concentrated on getting a job to pay for his condominium fees and expenses related to his car. He prepared a résumé that stressed his academic accomplishments, his language abilities, and his foreign travel. He sent copies—together with his college transcript—to members of Congress, business firms engaged in international trade, banks, and others. I referred him to friends of mine in government. He had numerous interviews, some of which seemed promising, but as summer turned to fall, no job was forthcoming. The graduates from all the colleges in the Washington area were scrambling for jobs, and the competition was fierce.

Our pastor referred Sean to the head of a real estate firm in Washington. After an interview, Sean was hired. It was a job for which he was overqualified, but he accepted it because he needed the income and none of the other prospects had materialized. Also, it provided him with group health insurance.

While delighting in his new apartment, he came to our house almost every day for meals or to bring his laundry.

In mid-October, Sean received one thousand pounds (about fifteen hundred dollars) from his grandmother in England. This improved his spirits! He used the money to buy furniture for his apartment.

Sean had a satisfactory checkup by his doctor in early December 1986. "Don't get a flu shot," the doctor warned, "because it could affect your immune system."

Sean's health remained reasonably good until the fall of 1987, when he told us he had been running a fever for two weeks and that his temperature soared as high as 104 degrees at night; that he had night sweats that drenched his bed and pillows; and that he had fever sores inside his mouth. His limbs ached, he suffered from diminished hearing and vision, headaches, dizziness, and nausea. He was so exhausted all the time that he had a hard time getting through the day.

Brenda and I had never seen our son's spirits so low. Although he didn't say it, he obviously thought he had clinical AIDS. He seemed to be preparing us for his demise and stunned us when he said, "I wish I were dead." This is shocking and distressing for any parent to hear. We hugged him and assured him we would always take good care of him.

Sean's friend Buddy told him the sores in his mouth were thrush, a kind of yeast infection that forms a white coating inside the mouth. "He gave me some lozenges which seemed to help even though they haven't been approved by the Federal Drug Administration," Sean informed us.

A few days later, he had an invitation from Buddy to go to Acapulco with him for five days. Sean was excited at the prospect, and, in view of his low spirits a week earlier, we encouraged him to go. He wrote a note to his employer, informing him that he would be away the following week. While he was on vacation, Sean called us several times, rhapsodizing about the beauty of Acapulco. "The lesions have gone from my mouth, and I haven't had a fever since we arrived here."

We went over to his apartment to see him when he returned around midnight. Looking tanned and well, he enthusiastically described the wonders of Acapulco until one-thirty in the morning. We were mystified that the trip did Sean such a world of good. It was much more beneficial than any medicine he received.

Three days later, his fever returned.

On the recommendation of Sean's specialist, he began to see a variety of experts for various aspects of his condition. The utter thoughtlessness of some of these doctors irritated me. I was distressed that when Sean was suffering from the pain and anxiety associated with his disease, he would often have to sit for an hour or more beyond his scheduled doctor's appointment in a windowless waiting room, where stale air was circulated by an inadequate air conditioner. Here, the only distraction was reading outdated *Time* magazines or medical journals containing technical articles punctuated with glossy ads for expensive foreign cars and cruises to exotic lands—glum reminders that the doctors' fees would probably far exceed the medical insurance Sean carried. Meanwhile, costs were mounting in the adjacent parking garage where exorbitant hourly fees were imposed on captive patients. Usually, when Sean was finally called by the nurse, he was shunted into a tiny examining room, where he waited for another fifteen or twenty minutes. Rarely, did a doctor take the few seconds necessary to say he was sorry for the delay. I found this uncaring attitude inexcusable.

Once, when one of Sean's specialists accepted a position in a distant city, Sean's case was assigned to another doctor. We arrived on time for the early morning appointment, but the new doctor kept Sean waiting for an hour. When he finally saw Sean, the doctor did not apologize for keeping him waiting. It was apparent that he had not read Sean's case history and that he was unfamiliar with his symptoms and how to treat them. We never went back to that doctor.

Everyone understands that doctors often have to treat emergency cases and that this throws off their scheduled appointments. But if this occurs, either the doctor or the nurse should take a minute to come out, apologize to the waiting patient, and explain the reason for the delay. I'm sure such a simple act of courtesy would serve to deflect the patient's mounting anger and frustration.

≈

I woke up from a nightmare at two-thirty one morning. I dreamed that Sean had died alone. Buddy was not with him, nor were we. I dreamt that I sent a cable to a friend in Paris, and another to my niece, saying that Sean had left this world. I got out of bed and went to my study and wept.

The next day, Sean called us at ten-thirty at night, saying he was lonely. "Come on over," I said. Without preliminaries, Sean said, "I know I'm dying, and I'm afraid I'll die in my sleep. Except for those five days in Mexico, my temperature has gone up to a hundred four degrees or higher every night for the past three weeks. The lesions have returned in my mouth, I've had terrible night sweats, and I'm always exhausted." Sean wept through much of this account.

"Two nights ago," he continued, "I dreamed I was in the hospital. You both were with me. Buddy was there, and so was Monsignor Benson. I knew I was on my deathbed." I was shaken by this and wondered, *Is God preparing us through dreams for Sean's death?*

Sean returned to his HIV specialist on November 19, 1987,

for blood tests. The specialist said, "I'm concerned about the thrush. It can be controlled if it's confined to the mouth, but it would be deadly if it got into the bloodstream. Don't have any dental work done, because even a routine cleaning would cause bleeding gums and carry the thrush into your bloodstream."

Then he expressed his concern about Sean's cough. He instructed Sean to have a chest X ray to determine if there was evidence of pulmonary pneumocystis. Finally, he said he was worried about Sean's high fevers.

When Sean got the results of his lab tests, the doctor told him that the AIDS virus was not overcoming the white blood cells. "That's the good news. The bad news is that the T4 count has dropped sharply, and I don't know how many of your T4 immune cells are active. Your X ray was normal," the doctor continued. "The scrapings of the lesions in your mouth were analyzed, and the results confirmed that you have thrush. This means that you have AIDS-related complex [ARC], but you don't yet have AIDS. I think you should start AZT, but you don't have to make this decision yet."

Sean was not eager to start taking AZT because of its unpleasant side effects. AZT is a powerful drug—and was the only one known to slow the progress of AIDS. Sean knew he would have to take it every four hours, twenty-four hours a day, every day and night for the rest of his life. "No," he insisted, "I don't want to start it."

I discussed this with Brenda. It was my feeling that Sean should take AZT to sustain him until a better drug came along. I could not give up hope that a miracle would happen to shield Sean from the ravages of AIDS. But as Brenda pointed out, "Sean fears the side effects of AZT. He's concerned that the anemia it causes would require repeated blood transfusions. He believes he has only a year or so to live anyway. If I were in his place, I'd probably not take the drug. Life under those conditions wouldn't be worth living."

When Sean came over that afternoon, we told him of our conversation. "I'm not ready for AZT," he said flatly. "The side effects scare me. It's easy for the doctor to recommend it, but *I'll* decide if and when I'm ready to start it."

And, of course, he was right.

I talked to Sean's specialist the next day. He told me that Sean's immune system had deteriorated faster than he anticipated. His T4 count had dropped from a normal 810 in September 1986 to 624 in September 1987, then plunged to 360 in just two months. "I'd like him to embark on a program of AZT, but I won't insist on it," he said. "Normally, AZT is started when the T4 count drops to two hundred. AZT will slow down further deterioration of the immune system, but it won't regenerate it. Its side effects are indigestion, fatigue, nausea, and headache. It causes a drop in the red-cell blood count but rarely sufficient to require blood transfusions. If excessive anemia does occur, the dosage can be adjusted. The usual dosage is one AZT tablet every four hours, twenty-four hours a day. The current cost of AZT is about seven hundred dollars a month, eighty percent of which should be covered by health insurance.

"If Sean declines to start AZT," the doctor warned, "he should anticipate a twenty-five to fifty percent chance of contracting AIDS in the next twelve months; and a seventy-five to ninety percent chance in the next twenty-four months."

I thanked the specialist for his frank, if grim, briefing on our son's condition. Sean was realistic about his bleak prospects, but sometimes his bitterness would break through. "Granny's in her nineties, and she keeps saying she wishes she'd die. I'm twenty-five and I want to live, but soon I'll be dead."

Later, when we were alone, Brenda confided, "If Sean dies,

I'll die, too, because we're so much a part of one another." I couldn't bear the thought of losing both of them.

I talked to Monsignor Benson and revealed to him that Sean was HIV positive. The monsignor was the first person we told. I felt we had to have someone outside the family whom we could talk to candidly about Sean's condition. Monsignor said that Sean meant a great deal to him and assured me that we could come to him at any time. He said he would pray for us all.

Blessed St. Joseph, born to be the guardian of Jesus the protector and consoler of Mary! Make powerful intercession for me, that my pious resolutions may not prove in vain; that I may be born to an interior and spiritual life that I may have such an increase of sanctity, so ardent a love of purity, so great a conviction of my own unworthiness, so clear a light of the emptiness and vanity of worldly grandeur, so as to esteem and relish only things that are eternal. Through our Lord Jesus Christ. Amen.
                    —A prayer from Sean's breviary

9

Sean had built a wall between us and his gay friends and companions, but we insisted he give us at least their first names and telephone numbers—and he did. We needed assurance that we could find him if we needed him or if we were worried about him.

We talked from time to time on the telephone with Buddy, with whom Sean had a longtime relationship. Buddy called Brenda on February 26, 1988, with an account about Sean that made us realize that something new and disturbing was happening to him. Buddy said that Sean told him his uncle was an Argentine general who had fought against the British in the Falkland Islands War and that he, Sean, was a major in the Argentine Army. Sean also told his companion he had two brothers in Argentina. He claimed his income was thirty thousand dollars a year, and that Brenda and I were worth $13 million. Sean's frequent visits to Buenos Aires and his fluency in the language made this story plausible to his friends. Aghast at this preposterous fabrication, Brenda quickly gave Buddy the facts. This was the first of a series of extraordinary flights of fancy that Sean told his friends and associates about himself. Our fears took on new proportions, and we had to admit to ourselves that apparently Sean's illness and his strong and diverse medications had affected his brain.

One day, Sean invited Buddy to come to Mass at our church, and we met our son's companion for the first time. He was a tall, slim man in his forties with a pleasant southern drawl. He told us he had four sisters, and he was the only boy in the family. He said that his mother and sisters all knew he was gay and that this was never a matter of contention in his family. And then he told us that he had been HIV positive since 1982.

We agreed to keep in regular touch with one another from then on. Buddy seemed to know a great deal about AIDS and its treatment, and we said we would like to see him again soon. In subsequent conversations and visits, Buddy provided us with a broader knowledge of Sean's condition, filling in for us a lot of gaps in our understanding of the illness up until that time. We were shocked when Buddy reported that Sean had been drinking heavily.

"Sean's favorite drink is Myer's rum mixed with 7-Up. In an evening out, he'll drink ten or twelve of these, saying he has a pain in his back so severe that he has to drink to ease the agony. We've got to do something," Buddy urged. Sean had first mentioned a pain in his back six weeks earlier, but the cause had not been determined.

We confronted our son about his excessive alcohol consumption and said we could arrange to get him into a hospital for treatment. He was furious and refused to have anything to do with this. "You can't control my life. I'm not thirteen years old anymore. I, and I alone, will decide if and when I go into treatment!" It was a fiery confrontation, after which he slammed out of the house.

Buddy called later to tell us that Sean had eventually calmed down but still remained opposed to the idea of treatment, repeating he was "not ready." We could see that Sean's drinking compounded his already monumental problems and probably contributed to his extravagant fantasies.

Buddy met us again at Mass the following Sunday, and we all had lunch together. Sean had only two or three forkfuls of Persian melon and a glass of ginger ale. He said he had not been able to keep food down for several days. Then we all discussed Sean's problem with alcohol. It was not an easy conversation by any means. Sean admitted that he had had "nine or ten" glasses of Myer's rum and tonic the previous Friday night. And he acknowledged that he had a serious problem, adding that if he started drinking again, he knew his relationship with Buddy would be in jeopardy—to say nothing of the effect it would have on Brenda and me.

"I haven't had a drink in thirty-six hours, and I have no desire for one. I'm not an alcoholic. I know I can stay away from it, and I will," Sean insisted. I made him promise that if he could not go without a drink, he would enter treatment. He agreed to attend a meeting of Alcoholics Anonymous (AA). This was a start; but neither Brenda, nor Buddy, nor I had much hope that Sean could stop drinking without professional help.

Buddy told us about the Whitman-Walker Clinic, a local organization that provided services for gays afflicted with AIDS. Brenda called the clinic and learned that it had an alcohol treatment program lasting sixteen weeks with two 2-hour sessions a week. Attendance at five AA meetings a week was obligatory. The entire program, including aftercare, lasted thirteen months and cost twenty dollars a week. Everyone in the program was gay, and many were HIV positive. We thought this option might be more appealing to Sean.

However, Sean continued to suffer from severe back pain. On March 15, his specialist gave him an injection of a medication called Bactrim to help alleviate his symptoms. It seemed to help temporarily, but the pain returned with a vengeance just a few days later.

A week afterward, Sean fell off the wagon. Buddy told us he had only one drink of rum, and "it blitzed him." He said Sean could hardly hold his head up. This violent reaction was doubtless due to the combination of alcohol and the new strong medication for his back pain.

After the Mass on Palm Sunday, Sean spent a couple of very pleasant hours with us. In a candid conversation about his sexual activity, he told us that he had been sexually active since he was sixteen, that is, since 1981. Brenda and I had been totally unaware of this. More than perplexing, it was deeply distressing and painful that we as parents didn't really "know" our son for all those years. In any event, I was impressed by the change I saw in him that day. He looked healthy, was smoking less, was amusing, and had a positive attitude. He talked of getting a better job after his vacation, and had even asked Monsignor Benson to keep him in mind if he learned of an interesting job opportunity. I credited this change in Sean to abstention from alcohol and the benefits of his new medication. We relished days like this when his spirits were high because we realized such days were gifts—and limited in number.

On Good Friday, Sean came over for lunch prior to the Stations of the Cross and returned after the service, tired after six-and-a-half hours of duty at Our Lady of Victory Church. After a pleasant visit, he returned to his apartment for an early night.

He awoke the following morning with a raging fever, but in spite of this, he went to church and conducted rehearsals for the altar servers in preparation for the long Easter Vigil Mass at which he would serve as well. After the Vigil, he returned home with us for dinner and stayed the night. He did not sleep well, though, and was up early to serve at the Easter Sunday Masses. It had been a grueling few days for him at Our Lady of Victory Church. But even as his health worsened, he continued to draw sustenance and strength from his faith and his service at our parish church. This prayer of John Henry Newman, I'm sure, was often on his lips:

> *May He support us all the day long*
> *till the shadows lengthen*
> *and the evening comes*
> *and the busy world is hushed*
> *and the fever of life is over*
> *and our work is done.*
>
> *Then,*
> *in his mercy*
> *may he give us safe lodging*
> *and a holy rest*
> *and peace at the last.*

Sean's physician recommended that he see another specialist for his back pain. The Bactrim was effective for only about six hours, after which the excruciating pain in his lower back would return. Sean looked so tired and tense. After an initial examination and a series of lab tests, the new specialist took biopsies that revealed that Sean had two types of viral infection: proctitis, which caused bleeding, a mucous discharge, and considerable pain; and cytomegalovirus (CMV).

"Of these," he said, "CMV is the more serious. CMV attacks the eyes and the lower intestinal tract. You have an excessive percentage of CMV in your blood cells, and while Bactrim can ease the pain and arrest the infection, it can't kill it, because CMV appears to be immune from antibiotics. Surgery is not indicated, and your immune system is so depleted that ganciclovir [Cytovene], a promising experimental treatment for CMV, would be inappropriate for you."

When we were alone later, Sean told us that one of Buddy's

friends had recently died of CMV. As far as Sean knew, there was no cure for it. His mood was subdued.

Sean reported the results of the biopsies to Buddy, who described the manifestations of CMV as they had affected his friend. "The virus turned the blood acidic," he said, "so much so that it caused blindness. Then it attacked the intestine, creating lesions affecting all body functions. Finally, the acid ate through the intestine, causing death. In my friend's case, CMV took six months from the time it was detected until he died."

This account distressed Sean, as he remembered that the pain in his lower back, the first indication of CMV, had started five months earlier. He wanted to stay close to his mother and me. He slept in our room next to Brenda—although quite restlessly because of his high fever.

In the middle of the night, Brenda sat bolt upright in bed and said, "Patchouli is the cure!"

"What's patchouli?" I asked. Brenda, who had been sound asleep, said she hadn't the faintest idea, but she heard a voice say this as she slept. Brenda's dreams and visions so often turned out to be true that she got out of bed and searched vainly for "patchouli" in her Russian dictionary. Meanwhile, I looked in my *Webster's Collegiate Dictionary* and, to my astonishment, found it. It was described as an East Indian mint yielding a fragrant essential oil.

How could a word we had never heard in our lives before actually exist and turn out to be a kind of herb? So many medications are derived from herbs. Could patchouli actually be the cure for AIDS or for CMV, which was so much on our minds? Perhaps a research scientist will explore this.

At a subsequent appointment with his new specialist, Sean learned that the CMV infection was spreading. We prayed for God's help. In the two years since Sean had been HIV positive, we had been on a roller coaster of emotions. Hopeful medical discoveries were dashed by increasingly serious manifestations of Sean's disease.

Sean begged us not to reveal to the parish that he was suffering from a "gay disease" for fear of losing their esteem and jeopardizing his work in the church that he loved so much. "If anyone asks," he said, "tell them I have cancer."

By respecting his wishes, we remained emotionally and physically boxed in. We had no relatives to whom we could turn, nor could we bring ourselves to bare our anguish to strangers in a support group. We could only turn to each other for support and to God for spiritual help.

The following prayer from Sean's breviary was written about this time:

> *Omnipotent Creator whose unerring providence adds joy every moment to the angels in heaven and to the saints upon earth, I most humbly beg, through the intercession of St. Joseph, that I may cheerfully acquiesce and rejoice in everything that comes from thy Fatherly hand; that I may be vigorous in executing Thy divine will and glorify thee in my present state.*
>
> *Grant me the true spirit of mortification to subdue my stubborn passions, to satisfy for what is past and to be a preservative from future dangers.*
>
> *Grant that my purity of intention, the meanest of my actions may be acceptable to Thee, as was the mite of the poor widow, which was put in the treasury in the temple.*
>
> *Through Jesus Christ our Lord. Amen.*

Brenda and I were having difficulty seeing our son suffer so, and not being able to speak to anyone else about it. Thank God we had each other to lean on. At the same time, Sean's courage and faith gave us strength—more than he'll ever know.

HOPE, AND
RESPITE,

10

After reading an article in *The Catholic Standard* about Medjugorje, in Bosnia and Herzegovina, where the Virgin Mary daily appears to children of the village, Brenda and I decided to look into the possibility of going there with Sean to seek Our Lady's help in dealing with our crisis. Deep in our hearts, we knew our only hope lay in a miracle. The next day I made reservations for the three of us to join a pilgrimage leaving on September 9, 1988, which was over two months away. We prayed that Sean would be able to make the trip.

When Sean told his friends of our plan to go to Medjugorje, one of them said that his secretary had been there five times and had returned with remarkable stories about the place. According to one story, a priest encountered an old man resting halfway up Cross Mountain. He asked if he could help, but the old man said he was determined to reach the top by the grace of God. He said he just needed to rest awhile longer. The priest went on to the top of the mountain. When he arrived, he was astonished to see the old man already there. In response to the priest's question, the man said that a friend had taken his arm and helped him to the top. The old man then opened his hand, on the palm of which was the face of Christ with the crown of thorns.

Another story concerned a family with two teenage children

on Apparition Hill, where Our Lady first appeared to the visionaries. The father took a photograph of the children playing with a Frisbee. When the film was processed back home, he was amazed to see the Virgin in the background between the two boys.

On July 13, Monsignor Benson had coronary triple bypass surgery, which fortunately was a success, and, ten days later, he was able to return to his apartment for a month, where his sister could take care of him. Sean, who worked closely with the priest every day, was deeply concerned, even while he continued to have problems of his own.

The intense pain in his back (actually the site of the CMV infection of his lower intestine) indicated that the Bactrim was no longer working.

Sean's twenty-fourth birthday came on July 23. We celebrated it quietly at home. He looked great in his white shorts and sports shirt. He was in a good mood that day, and we talked at length about our forthcoming pilgrimage to Medjugorje. Sean, inspired by what he had heard about Medjugorje, was looking forward to the pilgrimage. Secretly, though, Brenda and I could not help but wonder if this might be Sean's last birthday.

Buddy invited Brenda and me to his home, a house he had tastefully restored. While showing us a fountain he had built in his garden, he remarked soberly, "Sean is very sick and has a high fever most of the time. He's drinking less and eating hardly at all. It frightens me." Then he took us down to his basement, where he had set up a sewing workshop with long tables and three sewing machines. Here, with Buddy's help, people who had lost their loved ones to AIDS came to make cloth panels to commemorate their lives. These panels would be incorporated into the AIDS Quilt.

"My own health is deteriorating," Buddy confessed. "My T-cell count has dropped sharply. I think I'll die before Sean.

I've started making my own panel for the AIDS Quilt." (In fact, Buddy outlived Sean by about six months.)

The AIDS Quilt is part of the NAMES Project. It was started in San Francisco as a way for the companions or families of victims of AIDS to commemorate the life of their loved ones by embroidering a cloth panel with quotations, pictures, or other reminders describing the deceased. Like Buddy, some people with AIDS embroider their own panels.

Each panel measures three feet by six feet, the dimensions of a grave. The panels are then sewn together in thirty-two-panel squares and assembled to form the AIDS Quilt. Initially spread out on the Mall in Washington, D.C., the Quilt is now so large that it can no longer be displayed in its entirety. Portions of it are now on display in libraries, schools, and hospitals to keep alive public awareness of the expanding AIDS crisis.

During supper with Sean one evening in early August, we began to talk about our departure for Medjugorje on September 9. But Sean, who just a year earlier was planning his life's career, now said, I can't plan for anything a month in advance."

Early the next morning, he called us from his apartment and said he had only slept for an hour during the night and that he had a fever of 104.8 degrees. Despite our protests, he went to work anyway, but returned early, saying he had never felt so sick. He fell asleep on our couch, unable to climb the stairs to the bedroom.

Unable to confine our secret any longer, I went to the rectory and spoke with Monsignor Echle, one of our parish priests. (We didn't want to disturb Monsignor Benson during his convalescence.) I told him that Sean was terminally ill with AIDS. I described his state of health and said he would not be able to serve at Masses that weekend. Monsignor was both shocked and saddened. He said he would keep Sean in his prayers. Our circle of support had increased by one more.

That evening, Sean's temperature was 104.5 degrees. He complained of cramps in his calves, which he said he had had for three weeks. Then he spoke of experiencing sharp nerve spasms in his feet and fingers and said three fingers on his right hand were numb. Also, his hearing had deteriorated further. He said he did not know how much longer he would be working at the real estate firm, but he wanted to keep working at the rectory and serving Mass as long as possible.

Sean was asleep again when Buddy telephoned us later in the evening to urge us to take Sean to the hospital emergency room. I then called Sean's regular physician, who instructed us to keep giving Sean fluids to lower his fever and to call his CMV specialist in the morning. Our physician said it was essential to determine the cause for Sean's high fevers. Meanwhile, I called Sean's employer and explained that Sean would not return to work until his health improved.

Brenda, fearing Sean might die in the night, lay down on the floor next to him, cooling his fiery forehead with cold compresses. He slept restlessly most of the night, with spells of delirium, awaking from time to time to drink some ginger ale. His breathing was rapid and irregular.

I called the specialist at 6:00 a.m. When I described Sean's current symptoms, the doctor said that Sean's condition seemed to be out of control and he should be in the hospital. The specialist said he could see Sean at eleven-fifteen. (Later he told me that when he first heard my voice, he was sure I had called to tell him that Sean was dead.) There at his office on the morning of August 5, 1988, the doctor reiterated that Sean should be in the hospital so that a number of tests could be done, including a CAT scan to determine if he had lymphomic cancer. But Sean adamantly refused.

"Unless you go into the hospital for tests and treatment," the doctor warned, "you could die at any time." Sean still rebelled at the idea. "If you won't do it for yourself," Brenda interrupted, "do it for those of us who love you." At this plea, Sean relented. The doctor arranged for a hospital room, and we drove Sean there immediately.

He was put in a semi-private room in a wing reserved for patients with AIDS. When we arrived for a visit that evening, we noticed on the outside of the door a red sign warning visitors not to enter without first reporting to the nurses' station. There, to our dismay, we were instructed to put on sterile gloves from the glove box in his room before touching our son. This was absolutely unthinkable. We ignored the warning. We could not and did not put on gloves.

Later, when the doctor and nurse came in to examine Sean, Brenda and I made room for them by going over to talk to Sean's roommate, whom I'll name "Frank." He was very ill. His arms and face were marked with the distinctive Kaposi's sarcoma lesions. He had been in the hospital for two weeks; yet, tragically, no one had come to visit him. He was gaunt, coughed incessantly, and moaned, much to Sean's distress. We were really touched by Frank's condition and could not fathom how there could be *no one* at all who cared about his life. He said his family had cut him off and that his companion had left him. Frank told us he had only recently moved to Washington, and so no one here knew him. I told the head nurse about his plight.

A little later, a volunteer from Whitman-Walker Clinic, alerted by the nurse, was at Frank's bedside, talking to him quietly. The volunteer offered to help Frank make a will and write to his family. This was the first time I had seen the Whitman-Walker support system in action, and I was impressed.

When we returned to the hospital the next morning, Sean had just had a chest X ray, an EKG, and blood tests. An IV tube inserted in the back of his left wrist fed him dextrose. He said he was feeling much better. His specialist came in while we were there and reported that the chest X ray was OK, but that another one would be taken after Sean's dehydration had been remedied.

Then the specialist outlined his plan for Sean's stay in the hospital: "Sean is going to have two CAT scans, one of his skull and the other of his abdomen. A blood specialist is scheduled to extract and analyze Sean's bone marrow. These tests will take four or five days." We promised Sean he would not stay in the hospital a minute longer than was necessary to determine the reason for his high fevers. Then he would come home with us, and we would care for him. We sensed, though, that he was afraid he would never leave the hospital alive.

At noon the next day, he looked much better. He had had the CAT scan of his cranium that morning. The specialist who came to see him during our visit seemed satisfied at Sean's improvement. Then he confessed his earlier fear that Sean would die of a massive heart attack on the night of August 4. "I wish I had," said Sean.

That afternoon, "Frank" died. No one was with him, not even his parents. *How,* I wondered, *could they harden their hearts against their son because he was gay? Were they worried about what the neighbors would say? How could they justify their uncaring attitude when their son was stricken with this terrible affliction and died? What must their life be like now? Could they really continue to be self-righteous with the knowledge that they were not with their son when he needed their love and support the most?* I simply cannot understand this attitude, yet it is the unfortunate situation in too many families.

Sean said earnestly, "Don't let me die in the hospital like Frank did." We promised him we would not let that happen. Then he cried out in desperation, "I just *have* to get home!"

The floor nurse arrived just then to take his pulse and temperature. She put a thermometer in his mouth while she took his pulse, then turned to make a notation on his chart. Sean, with an impish expression, took advantage of her inattention and quickly popped his thermometer into the pitcher of ice water, returning it to his mouth just as she turned back to him. When she removed the thermometer and read it, she asked, "Have you had any water to drink recently?" "No," he replied honestly. She made another notation on his chart and left the room. Sean winked at his mother.

His specialist came back that evening again and, after reviewing all of Sean's charts and available test results, said he would release him from the hospital with the proviso that he not work for a week. Then he took me to one side, out of the hearing of Brenda and Sean, and said, "The cranium CAT scan revealed that Sean's brain has atrophied. This will manifest itself in the next year or two as premature aging. I didn't tell this to Sean because he's already burdened with so many problems. I understand Sean's despair about his bleak future," he continued. "Inevitably, he will be stricken with other opportunistic infections."

That's what I respected about Sean's specialist. He never pulled his punches.

After giving us aftercare instructions, the doctor added that he was not at all sure that Sean would be well enough to go to Medjugorje on September 9.

We took Sean home with us. Once we were out of the hospital and he had a cigarette, his spirits soared. Later, when we were alone, I told Brenda what the specialist had said about the deterioration of Sean's brain.

Buddy called on August 9 and suggested that Sean was qualified to retire on a disability and claim Social Security payments. And the AIDS representative at the Social Security office assured me that Sean was indeed eligible to receive benefits immediately. In addition, he might be eligible to receive Medicaid benefits, which would cover all medical bills and prescriptions. Then, after five months, he would be eligible for Social Security Disability Insurance (SSDI).

I also talked to the Social Security representative at the Whitman-Walker Clinic, who assured me that Sean's group health-insurance benefits would continue for eighteen months, provided he continued to pay the premiums.

This information was heartening. I felt as if some weight had been lifted from my shoulders.

Sean, who had remarked in the past that he was having a problem with his eyesight—especially his depth perception—finally, at my urging, had his eyes examined and bought prescription glasses. He was astonished to note how much better he could see with them.

Shortly after this, a new complication arose—but this time it had nothing to do with Sean. It was the return of a back problem I had suffered periodically ever since World War II. After straining my back a few days earlier, I was now wearing a back brace. The acute pain made walking so difficult that I had to use a cane most of the time.

I went to an orthopedist, who diagnosed the problem as sciatica and ordered five days of bed rest. He prescribed three medications, and he urged us to postpone our pilgrimage to Medjugorje. But there was no way that I was going to spend five days in bed; I still had to take care of Sean. So I just rested whenever I could in between.

Despite his high fever, Sean wanted to serve at the Saturday evening Mass. We could not dissuade him. Even on Sunday, he was determined to serve at the eight o'clock Mass, but when he genuflected at the altar, he felt dizzy and weak. He barely managed to hang on, but nevertheless continued serving until the end of Mass.

Sean's physical condition was going from bad to worse. He had raging fevers that caused night sweats leading to dehydration. To restore fluids to his system, Sean's specialist ordered daily intravenous infusions of dextrose in a saline solution. At night, Sean was sometimes delirious. His pulse was extraordinarily high, and nothing seemed to help rid him of the thrush. He underwent several transfusions a week to enrich his blood, but he never complained. He dealt with this AIDS nightmare with remarkable courage and tenacity to live. His demeanor was an example to Brenda and me to hold on and to deal with each crisis as it arose—one at a time.

It was obvious that Sean could no longer live at his own apartment. The time had come for home-care nursing. Since he slept on the couch in our living room, the nurse, Cathy Parrish, set up an IV kit there to counteract Sean's high fevers and dehydration. As she did so, she began to teach us nursing skills. Because Brenda had arthritis in her fingers, the responsibility for most aspects of Sean's medical care fell to me.

The nurse installed a catheter in Sean's left arm and showed me how to set up a sterile tray, to use sterile gloves, to connect the tube from the bottle of dextrose-saline to the catheter, and, finally, how to disconnect the IV. She said she would replace the catheter herself every seventy-two hours.

The next morning at six-thirty, I connected the IV again. After the bottle was empty, I disconnected it as I was taught. I was gaining more confidence to deal with all the procedures. (When the nurse arrived to change the catheter, she watched with approval as I attached the bottle, the tube, and the needle.) When Sean next saw his specialist, he was told that his spleen was enlarged, which could account for his high fevers. The bone-marrow biopsy was normal. The doctor drew blood for a T4, T8 count and said he would have the results in three days. Then he instructed us to continue the IV daily to combat dehydration.

By this time, Sean had decided to quit his job at the real estate firm. Because he was in no condition to do so himself, I went to Sean's office and told his employer that Sean was too ill to continue working there. Sean's boss expressed sincere regret and gave me three back paychecks for Sean, as well as a box containing his belongings. While there, I arranged to pay the monthly premiums for Sean's group health insurance. I was assured that his coverage would remain in force as long as the firm retained group coverage and we paid the premiums. When I left, his employer said he would pray for Sean.

Three days later, Sean's specialist called to say that Sean's T4 count had dropped to 197. "It's time for Sean to start taking AZT," he suggested. "I don't know how he will feel in two weeks' time, so I recommend that you cancel your pilgrimage to Medjugorje. I also think he should see a neurologist about the numbness in his feet."

Reluctantly, I canceled our pilgrimage to Medjugorje.

At Sean's next appointment, his specialist put him on a regime of AZT. He prescribed two capsules every four hours around the clock—double the dosage he previously indicated would be necessary!

Since we had never held secrets from Sean, we told him the truth: that his high fevers had caused damage to his brain, which, according to his specialist's reading of the cranium CAT scan, probably would not manifest itself for a while. Sean was understandably disturbed at this news, but he took it very well. He speculated that this condition was probably responsible for his lapses in memory.

After a series of tests, the neurologist recommended by Sean's specialist determined that Sean's pain and numbness in both feet was caused by neuropathy, a degenerative state of the nerves. "Which," he explained, "causes the disintegration of the protective covering of the nerves. Without this protection, even a gentle touch will cause great pain. This is a common symptom of HIV."

On August 30, our wedding anniversary, Sean wrote us this heartwarming card:

> To the most loving parents imaginable:
> Happy anniversary!
> You have always been there to love me and
> take care of me for the last 24 years.
> Thank you so much for being the perfect parents.
> With much love,
>
> *Sean*

The card brought tears to our eyes. Needless to say, we kept it along with his other cards and letters we so treasure.

On September 1, for the first time in months, Sean's temperature fell to subnormal. Brenda asked him if there was anything he wanted—anything at all. He replied instantly, "I want a little dog, a miniature black-and-tan dachshund." Sean went on to specify that he wanted a dog exactly like the one belonging to our neighbor, who walked him by our house every day.

A friend drove Brenda down to a kennel located near Richmond, while I took care of Sean. When she returned, she held in her arms a tiny black-and-tan dachshund puppy, just twelve weeks old, weighing about three pounds. He was alert, intelligent, and affectionate. Sean was absolutely delighted. He named the puppy "Cesare."

When Cesare wasn't into everything, he stayed close to us, playing happily or sleeping. But it wasn't long before he could jump up on the couch to be with Sean. Often, he clambered over Sean's feet, causing him excruciating pain. To train Cesare not to do this, I tried locking him out on the porch, but he whined, then yapped incessantly until we let him back in. In an effort to establish some measure of control, I attached a lightweight leash to his collar. But that didn't work well, either. So we decided to take him to an obedience school. I assumed that after the usual six-week course he would return to us an "obedient" dog. The trainer made it clear, however, that if Cesare was ever going to respond to our commands, we would have to be trained as well. This meant that both Brenda and I had to leave Sean three times a week for an hour each time. We were distracted during these training sessions, worrying about our son. As a result, when training was completed, Cesare obeyed all the trainer's commands and paid little attention to ours!

When I attempted to register "Cesare" with the American Kennel Club, I discovered that name had already been taken. So I settled for "Little Caesar," naming him after the gangster role played by Edward G. Robinson in a movie of that name in the 1930s. Eventually, we abbreviated his name to "Caesar." The little dog sensed that Sean was ill and comforted him by staying by his side. (Now that Sean is gone, Caesar is our constant companion.)

Understandably, Sean was now becoming increasingly impatient with lab tests, the IV, endless appointments with doctors—and the bad news they brought him.

In face of all the difficult realities about his condition, Sean tried his best to live as full a life as possible. And his mother and I tried to allow him as much "latitude" as was possible and prudent. He attempted to drive his car, but this proved unwise because of his poor coordination and depth perception. Whenever he felt strong enough, he served at Mass, even though he had officially resigned as sacristan by this time. Occasionally, he went out to dinner in restaurants with Buddy, knowing he probably could not keep food down. Between Sean's transfusions, he and Buddy went to the beach in Maryland. Once they even went to North Carolina for a few days to visit with friends.

In the fall of 1988, Sean and Buddy went to an AIDS benefit. They were seated at the same table as a prominent AIDS researcher who expressed his astonishment at the solidarity, strength, and affluence of the gay community. He said he could not believe, from looking at Sean, that he had AIDS. It would seem that working in his laboratory afforded him little, if any, direct contact with people actually infected with the disease for which he was seeking a cure.

The AIDS researcher described to Sean and Buddy a promising new treatment called soluble CD4, which he and his colleagues were working on at the National Institutes of Health. He explained that soluble CD4 attached itself to the AIDS virus and "sponged it up," thus preventing it from binding to the CD4 molecule on the surface of the T4 cells. This would then block infection of the cells.

On the face of it, soluble CD4 seemed to be an interesting development; but in Sean's case, it would neither cure him nor prolong his life because it did not regenerate T4 cells. Sean's immune system was already so depleted that even if soluble CD4 blocked the AIDS virus from attacking his few remaining T4 cells, he still could not combat an infection.

When Sean was too weak or ill to go to church, Monsignor Benson brought him Communion at our home. Brenda and I left them alone, and they talked together earnestly, often for at least an hour. In the latter part of November, Sean felt strong enough to accompany us to a novena at our church. There, he was greeted warmly by the parishioners. They evidently knew that Sean was gravely ill: His face was gaunt and his body thin. His weight had dropped to 128 pounds, a loss of ten pounds in fourteen days.

On those increasingly rare days when he had no fever and his neuropathy was not too painful, Sean's spirits rose and his sense of humor returned. We all relished these days and the needed respite they provided. One night, when the medication seemed to be controlling the CMV and Sean felt well enough to do things around the house, he polished the brass andirons, a brass Indian tray, some copper pans, and a brass Indian statue. On another occasion, he woke up in the small hours of the morning and cleaned the marble top of the coffee table. These activities took his mind off his problems, and we were glad for such occasional bouts of initiative.

When Sean was at Buddy's house one evening, he had a rum drink before taking two Dilantin pills for his neuropathy. Within a few minutes, his face turned bright red, his fever shot up to 106 degrees, and Buddy put him to bed. Sean was violently ill all night long. By morning, fortunately, his temperature had dropped to 103 degrees.

The next day, Sean's neuropathy was worse than it had ever been, affecting both legs, both hands, and his neck. "I feel," he said, "as if my body is rusting."

I tried to keep my feelings hidden inside, but it was terrible to see Sean like this. Despite his youth, he moved like an old man. I prayed all the harder for divine help to rid Sean of this dire affliction.

Meanwhile, Buddy was dealing with his own AIDS crisis. One evening he told Sean, "My Ampligen program has been canceled and this could have a serious adverse effect on my health." His fear was confirmed three days later, when he learned that his T4 count had dropped to 400. He decided he could not stay in Washington for another harsh winter, so he went back home to Georgia to be with his mother for a while, then on to Florida. This was a severe blow to Sean, who had come to depend on Buddy's company and support. But Buddy promised to invite Sean to join him in Florida for a week or ten days.

I was disappointed that President-Elect George Bush had not made a public statement recognizing the gravity of the AIDS crisis. I had known him when he was the director of the CIA and I was the national intelligence officer for Latin America. After I retired in 1980, we kept in contact with each other. One day, I sent him a copy of *The Quilt*, a picture book displaying thousands of panels spread out on the Mall in Washington in memory of AIDS victims.

Along with the book, I sent him this letter:

5 December 1988

Dear President-Elect Bush:

This book, *The Quilt*, brings home with compassion and poignancy the wrenching despair the AIDS tragedy has on the families and friends of tens of thousands who have been stricken with this dread disease and died. As those infected multiply, the entire nation will become frightened and saddened.

Even if you only read a page or two at a time, I will feel more comfortable knowing that the President of the United States has this book, has read it and recognizes the urgency of resolving this crisis.

With best wishes.

Respectfully,

Robert Hopkins

Four days later I received this reply:

THE VICE PRESIDENT
WASHINGTON

December 9, 1988

Mr. Robert Hopkins
2226 48th Street, N.W.
Washington, D.C. 20007

Dear Mr. Hopkins:

        Thank you for taking the time to write and for
the copy of "The Quilt." In turning the first few pages
I was able to see the human devastation caused to the
victims, as well as to their families and friends.

        Like you, I recognize the paramount importance of
finding a cure and vaccine to help control the spread of
AIDS. Our Administration has proposed dramatically
increasing federal resources for AIDS research and
education. In the 1989 budget, we requested that such
funding be increased by almost 35 percent, to $1.3 billion.
Our nation's commitment to the fight against AIDS must be
wholehearted -- and it must endure.

        I am very grateful for your kind words. Again,
my thanks for writing and best wishes.

                              Sincerely,

                              George Bush

While I was pleased to receive this letter, President Bush never
publicly expressed his concern about the AIDS crisis. Nevertheless, I kept writing to him in the hope that I could persuade
him to take a public stand on this vital issue, but unfortunately
my efforts failed.

11

Every August during the 1950s, when Brenda and I lived in France, we rented the Vieux Château, a thirteenth-century fortified castle overlooking the Mediterranean. Built to protect the villagers from Saracen raids from North Africa, it was situated above a mountain village.

This castle was the seat of power of a noble family who ruled a vast region of Provence, encompassing fifty cities and towns. In the latter part of the sixteenth century, the château was attacked, pillaged, and burned by a neighboring nobleman, only to be rebuilt, then pillaged again during the French Revolution. It gradually fell into ruin until restoration began in 1913. By 1924, it was again livable.

Now protected by the French government, it was declared a historic monument in 1931, which meant that the exterior could not be altered and any reconstruction or restoration had to be done under the supervision of experts from the National Fine Arts Commission.

From the outside, the château appeared to be still a ruin, but the inside had been carefully restored. The floors throughout were of Moroccan tile, each room having a different pattern. The walls and doors in the great room, the circular library, and the entry hall were oak-paneled. In the master bedroom, the paneling was carved in the linen pattern. It was completely furnished and had modern plumbing and central heating.

Across the courtyard was a watchtower, which in the 1950s was still in its ruined state. Whenever Saracens were sighted coming across the Mediterranean during the Dark Ages, a bonfire would be lighted on top of the watchtower to warn fortresses in either direction along the coast that a raid was imminent. There, in turn, other bonfires were lighted so that the entire coastline was alerted. This would signal the villagers to come inside the walls for protection.

It was a lovely, tranquil spot with gorgeous views of the mountains and the sea. A housekeeper came in during the day to clean the place and run errands. When she left, we had the château and the grounds to ourselves. The housekeeper and some villagers, however, were superstitious about the château, believing it to be haunted, and so they would not set foot in it after dark.

In the latter part of the fifteenth century, when the Black Plague ravaged Europe, the ailing king of France, Louis XI, summoned a renowned healer from southern Italy, a monk named Francesco Martotillo de Paule, founder of the religious order of Minimes ("The Least Ones"). Louis XI sent a ship to Calabria to carry François de Paule, as he became known, to France. He was refused permission to land at Marseilles and at Toulon, because those ports were quarantined to prevent the spread of the plague. He finally managed to land at a small fishing port between Toulon and St. Raphael, where fishermen welcomed him.

François blessed them, and they led him up the mountainside to the village, where there was a funeral cortege for a twelve-year-old girl who had just died from the plague. When François put his hand on the body of the child, she was restored to life. Those present, awed by this miracle, spread the word swiftly through the village, until it reached the nobleman at the château.

The nobleman invited François to be his guest at the château, and he remained there for several days.

Impressed by the warmth of his reception and the piety of the villagers, François, responding to a plea from the nobleman, prayed for God's mercy in ridding the village of the plague. His prayer was answered, and from that moment on, no one in the village died of the disease. Promising the inhabitants the benefit of his prayers forever, François then went on to care for the French king at the royal palace at Plessis les Tours.

François de Paule was canonized a saint by Pope Leo X on May 1, 1519. In 1560, he became the patron saint of the village, where a chapel was built and named for him. In 1654, the Vieux Château was turned over to the Order of Minimes and served as a monastery until the French Revolution.

When Sean was a boy, we told him countless stories about the château and showed him photographs we had taken of it in the years before he was born. He was so enchanted, he longed to see it himself. Brenda and I agreed that given the place's history (not to mention its beauty and tranquillity), a trip there might do our son a world of good. In December 1988, we decided the time had come. I wrote to the owner and told him that our son, who was terminally ill, wanted to see the château before he died. I arranged to rent it for two weeks in February 1989.

Over the winter, Sean and Buddy kept in touch by telephone. During one conversation, Buddy mentioned that a friend of his had been hospitalized because his neuropathy caused an infection that did not respond to antibiotics. Unfortunately, gangrene set in, and his leg was amputated. Sean was visibly shaken by this news. He asked me to buy him a footbath with a vibrator to stimulate circulation in his feet and prevent anything like this from ever happening to him. I bought him a footbath the next morning. (Horror accounts like this circulated freely among people with AIDS.)

Sean then made arrangements to fly to Fort Lauderdale on January 20 to be with Buddy for ten days. Buddy paid half the cost of his ticket, as his Christmas present to Sean. He called us every day: He was swimming and sunbathing on the beach, basking in 78-degree weather. It was a welcome change for him from the snow and cold of Washington.

Sean returned from Florida on January 30, looking healthy and tanned but noticeably disenchanted with Buddy. He did not confide in us about what had occurred between him and Buddy; and we didn't pry.

In contrast to the weather on January 1, the sun came out and the temperature rose to 76 degrees on February 1. We took this as a good omen. We were anxiously awaiting our trip to France. While Sean was in Florida, I had picked up our visas at the French embassy.

Before our departure, Sean saw his specialist again and got new prescriptions for all the medications he would need while we were in France. He also drew blood for a T4 count, saying he would report the results before our departure. Then Brenda, Sean, and I drove out to Maryland to look at the kennel where Caesar would stay while we were gone. We were pleased with the facilities and the personnel and convinced ourselves that Caesar would be as happy there as anywhere, but we knew he would miss us terribly.

Three days later, the specialist called me with the results of Sean's blood tests on February 2, comparing them to his previous tests on December 30. He said his T4 count dropped from 184 to 114, that Sean had no toxic effects from AZT, and that he should keep up his present dosage. "The French have a casual attitude about germs," he continued, and warned us that "Sean should have no aged cheeses. He should avoid paté, seafood, and other uncooked foods."

We packed on February 9, taking only what luggage we could

carry on the plane with us. (Years before, we had the unfortunate experience of losing our checked luggage when we arrived in Lisbon. We vowed then never to travel with more luggage than we could carry aboard the plane.)

After picking up our travelers' checks, I spent the remaining days before our departure in lengthy discussions with the Social Security office concerning Sean's Medicare and Medicaid coverage, as well as with his private health-insurance providers. We left satisfied that his health coverage was all in order.

After a grueling flight with two stopovers, we rented a car for the two-and-a-half-hour drive westward to the château. Despite our fatigue, our excitement grew as we approached the village and spotted the château above it.

"Prince," a mixed collie belonging to the housekeeper, greeted us at the gate. We became friends immediately. He stayed close by Sean throughout our stay, and Sean loved the extra company. We noticed only subtle changes in the château since we had last stayed there three decades before. The courtyard had been paved with flagstones, and the watchtower had been restored and converted to private apartments for the owner. Quarters for the housekeeper had been built within the walls so as not to alter the exterior. The garden, neglected during our previous visits, had been taken in hand and was filled with brilliant flowering plants and shrubs. The great umbrella pine at the gateway and other trees on the property had grown almost imperceptibly. The surrounding mountainsides were covered in brilliant yellow mimosas.

Inside, a new bathroom had been added. The furnishings were the same as we remembered, but some needed reupholstering. Likewise, the books on the shelves were the ones I remembered, as were the paintings on the walls. We felt as if we had returned "home."

Though very tired, Sean eagerly explored every room. He even climbed the spiral staircase to the ramparts overlooking the village and the sea. After lunch, he sunbathed in the court-yard and slept. The setting reminded me of the Garden of Gethsemane, which I had visited when I was about Sean's age. The words of the Twenty-third Psalm came to mind as I gazed at my son.

> The LORD is my shepherd;
> I shall not want.
> He maketh me to lie down in
> green pastures; he leadeth me
> beside the still waters.
> He restoreth my soul: He leadeth
> me in the paths of righteousness
> for his name's sake.
> Yea, though I walk through the
> valley of the shadow of death, I
> will fear no evil: for thou art
> with me; thy rod and thy staff
> they comfort me.
> Thou preparest a table before me in the
> presence of mine enemies: thou
> anointest my head with oil; my cup
> runneth over.
> Surely goodness and mercy shall
> follow me all the days of my life;
> and I will dwell in the house of the
> Lord forever.

That evening after supper, Brenda and Sean played back-gammon while I read a newly published book on the history of the village and the château. In it was an account of an attack on the château on the night of February 13, 1589, in which the nobleman and his brother were murdered in the great room.

The attackers then went on to pillage and burn the château. I felt a chill as I read this passage aloud to Brenda and Sean. The attack had taken place in the very room in which we sat that night, precisely four hundred years later.

I had worried that Sean, with his neuropathy, would have difficulty climbing the steep path between the village and the château. But after a good night's rest, he made the trip two or three times as he explored the beautiful ancient village, buying postcards, bread, cheese, paté, and wine. He chose to ignore his specialist's warnings, seeing no reason to deprive himself of his favorite foods. "In my condition," he quipped, "what else can happen to me?" The fact is, he thrived during our stay there, getting stronger each day. Not once did he have a fever or nausea or any of the symptoms he experienced back in Washington. His neuropathy, too, was much less severe than it had been at home.

The weather, luckily, was warm enough for us to go swimming, and Sean took every advantage of this. I held his hand while he painfully negotiated the narrow band of pebbles before stepping onto the sloping fine sand and into the water. After each swim and before he got out of the water, I would clear a path through the pebbles so he could walk on firm sand without discomfort.

During our stay, there was a daylong village festival celebrating the 200th anniversary of the French Revolution. A special Mass was followed by a strident hunting-horn concert in the courtyard of the church. A band of musicians led a parade of imaginative, mimosa-laden floats in fantastic shapes up the narrow, winding streets to the village square. Here and throughout the village, houses were decorated with French flags and bunting. After the floats were admired and prizes awarded to the most original, the inhabitants, old and young, all dressed in colorful costumes of the French Revolution, plucked the yellow blossoms from the floats for a battle of flowers.

After nightfall, the mayor, wearing his sash of office, offered local wine *gratis* to all comers, and there was dancing in the street under strings of multicolored lights. In the background, the Vieux Château, illuminated for the event, loomed against the dark sky.

It was an unexpected and delightful event that went on all day and well past midnight. Sean thoroughly enjoyed the spectacle, but he was tired as we climbed the steep hill to the château.

The following day, we drove through olive groves, vineyards, and villages to visit Saint-Tropez, a town that we had enjoyed very much years before. No sooner had we arrived than a sudden storm struck from the East with great force, drenching us with rain and buffeting us with high winds. So strong was the wind that we had difficulty keeping our footing. We made our way to Senéquier's café, where we had croissants, warm from the oven, and café au lait. Here we watched the boats in the port, bobbing up and down as the wind whistled through the rigging. The storm forced us to abandon the idea of shopping, and we returned to the security of the château, with its comforting stone walls, four feet thick.

Aside from trips down into the village and shopping in the street markets, we spent the remainder of our vacation at the château. There seemed to be no other place as pleasant as this. We were awed at the spectacular beauty of sunrise and sunset. At night, so far were we from the lights of the city that the stars stood out with great clarity, and we could watch the satellites that we and the Russians had launched move silently across the bowl of the dark sky.

Sean's health improved so dramatically during our stay that I could not help but think that Saint François de Paule had a hand in his recovery. With this in mind, I called the owner of the château before we left, requesting the opportunity to rent it again in the fall. He set aside two weeks for us in October.

12

Sean's good health continued long after we returned to Washington. He had gained weight in the South of France, and when his specialist tested his blood, the T4 and T8 counts had not diminished. Sean seemed to have unlimited energy. I dared to think that maybe he *could* beat this, maybe there *would* be a miracle.

He immediately began to spruce up his apartment by painting the kitchen. At night, he planned the menu for a dinner he would be serving for a couple of good friends on March 8. He decided to serve smoked salmon on toast points, filet mignon in the typical Argentine *chimichuri* sauce, potato-and-onion casserole, green salad, chocolate mousse, and coffee. All of which would be accompanied by Argentine wines. Obviously, he had inherited his mother's culinary skills. His dinner turned out to be a great success. He even showed his friends the dozens of photographs I had taken during our stay at the château.

While Sean's health was good and his spirits were high, my back pain returned with a vengeance. It virtually incapacitated me. On March 18, I had surgery for the removal of a fragment of a disk that had become dislodged and was pressing against the sciatic nerve. The surgery was successful, and I was able to walk without pain for the first time in months. Thankfully, this happened at a time when Sean's own condition was not in reverse.

The following week, Sean encountered Buddy at a black-tie fund-raiser for AIDS. "He's very ill," Sean later told us. "He's lost weight and is anemic because of taking AZT. He was out of breath just crossing the street and could hardly climb the stairs. I thought he was going to have a heart attack—I don't think he'll live much longer." Sean was concerned, but clearly was not going to resume his previous relationship with Buddy.

It was now early April. Sean, pleased at how much his kitchen was improved by painting and, possibly under the influence of spring fever, decided to repaint our front door and polish the brass fittings. The result was dazzling.

On April 10, Brenda announced that, for her own peace of mind, she had to go to Medjugorje. Knowing how strongly she felt, I arranged for her to join a pilgrimage leaving on April 21, returning on the twenty-ninth. I assured her that I would take good care of Sean while she was away and that he would eat well.

I knew that Medjugorje was a tiny remote village with little in the way of modern communications and that it would be unlikely we could stay in touch with one another during the time Brenda was there. This was the first time we had been apart in years, and I missed her immediately.

By this time, Sean had a new friend named Don about whom he was enthusiastic. Don had invited Sean out to dinner the evening Brenda left, so I had only Caesar for company. The house seemed huge and empty.

The next day, Sean and I decided to paint the attic as a surprise for Brenda. I spackled cracks, while Sean painted. At midafternoon, we broke for a lunch of delicious lasagna that Brenda had made for us before leaving. Then we took a brief outdoor "break." Our garden was breathtaking. We admired the scores of azaleas in various hues, the wisteria heavy with blossoms, and our cherry tree in full bloom.

Sean brought his new friend, Don, over to meet me on April 26. He had told me about Don's kindness and consideration, but I knew little else. A tall and solidly built man with thick hair and a mustache, Don was in his mid-forties and had worked at the Department of Labor for a number of years.

In meeting Don, I could perceive another dimension in Sean's life. What had been only a name became a mature personality, a man of strength who proved to have integrity as well. I sensed that he would take good care of Sean.

Brenda returned on the evening of April 29. Sean, Caesar, and I went to meet her. As we drove home, Brenda described her remarkable experiences in Medjugorje. She said a pilgrim in her group, a terribly emaciated man, was so weak when they arrived in Medjugorje that Brenda helped him off the bus and across the street. She carried his bag because he was not strong enough to carry it himself. He told her he was a hemophiliac who had received numerous blood transfusions. She was convinced he had AIDS. A day later, though, he was much better. By the second day, he became vigorous and was more active in walking and in climbing Cross Mountain than anyone else in the group. And he attended every Mass.

At St. James Church, the first evening, Brenda saw a flock of birds, chirping wildly and hurling themselves against the window to the choir loft where Our Lady appeared nightly to the young visionaries. The birds came at six-forty, when the Virgin appeared. Other pilgrims told Brenda that the birds did this every evening. The birds have even broken the window, and some fly about inside the church.

The pastor of St. James, impelled to document the miracles of Medjugorje, had each visionary write down the Virgin's message that was given each evening before they had an opportunity to discuss it among themselves. They passed the messages to the priest. Invariably, all the messages written down on the slips of paper were identical.

Brenda made the very difficult climb to the summit of Cross Mountain. There was no path, and the only handholds were the sharp-edged rocks of the mountain itself. The thorny shrubs that grew along the way made grabbing hazardous. Some of the pilgrims, in penance, made the climb barefooted.

The visionaries, to whom the Virgin first appeared in 1982 when they were children, were in their teens or early twenties during Brenda's visit. They spoke to groups of pilgrims, reporting their experiences and the messages Our Lady gave them.

Brenda returned home renewed and invigorated by this remarkable spiritual experience. We continued to pray for a miracle.

Sean's health improved even more, and with the return of his strength he took on the strenuous task of clearing the brush off our hill so I could plant vegetables and flowers there. In May, he decided to find another job and sent out his résumé to a couple of promising leads. He even thought of starting his own business. He and I began going to the exercise room in his apartment building for a daily workout. He was much more energetic than I, and so it was almost impossible to believe that he literally had been at death's door nine months before.

His good health enabled me to get back to activities I had pushed aside in order to care for him. I recorded for Georgetown University an oral history of my activities during World War II and my contacts with Allied wartime leaders. I also resumed writing on my memoirs and was able to devote more time to the Harry Hopkins Public Service Institute, of which I was president. We all worked together when it came to planting our gardens. Our lives had returned to normal.

By this time, Brenda had met Don and felt an immediate affinity for him. There was something about his quiet strength that inspired confidence. Little by little, we learned more about him. He had worked in the Peace Corps in India and had served in the Vietnam War.

Brenda and I talked it over one evening and decided that Sean would enjoy our next vacation at the château even more if Don came along, too. So we told Sean he could invite Don to stay in the château with us in October. Sean was delighted, and Don was overwhelmed. He accepted with pleasure and immediately began to study French after work.

On a routine visit to his specialist on June 9, Sean learned his weight had dropped from 142 pounds to 136 pounds. The doctor told him he *must* gain it back.

13

Brenda was concerned about her aging mother, Doris, who had recently been robbed. So, in July, Brenda went to visit Doris in England for a week. Brenda's cousin Rosemary met her when she arrived and drove her fifty miles to her mother's home. On the way, she told Brenda that her mother's condition had seriously deteriorated.

Doris had lived alone since her husband's death years before. She would not have a telephone in the house, claiming, "I don't need one, wouldn't use it if I had one, and I can't hear on the thing anyway." She said if she needed anything, she had only to use her cane to bang on the common wall between her house and that of her neighbor, whose husband would do anything for her. Doris could be very stubborn.

On July 23, Sean's twenty-fifth birthday, he had breakfast with me after Mass. I gave him an album for all the photographs from Brenda and me. Brenda called from England to wish Sean a happy birthday and told us about the night her mother was robbed. Brenda said the thief got in through the kitchen window. Doris was asleep but woke up when he was in her bedroom, rummaging through her things. She grabbed her cane, which she always kept next to her, let out a yell, and went after him with it. He managed to escape. Despite her age, Doris could be a vigorous and fierce woman.

She didn't like to use her hearing aid, so she claimed that was the only thing he stole.

The next morning, Rosemary came over with her seven-year-old son, Ben. He was excited about the events of the previous night. After examining the footprints on the wet ground outside the kitchen window, he came in and announced in his strong Lancashire accent, "Well, we know a good bit about the thief. First of all, he's got big feet, and we know he's deaf because he stole her hearing aid!"

Over the next few days, Sean had fever and night sweats. His temperature ranged from 102 to 103 degrees. He took aspirin to control his fever, but he also experienced waves of dizziness and nausea. Concerned that Sean's fevers and stomach problems signaled a return to last year's crisis, I took him to his specialist. Sean's weight had now dropped to 132 pounds. His doctor said that he must gain back five pounds before his next appointment on August 24 or he would put him back in the hospital.

Sean and I met Brenda at the airport on the afternoon of July 25. She had with her a little freckled-faced boy with red hair, who I assumed had traveled alone on the plane. But I was wrong. He was Ben, Rosemary's son.

The day before leaving England, Brenda said casually to Rosemary, "Perhaps someday Ben could come and visit us in Washington." "Do you mean that?" asked Rosemary. "Of course," said Brenda. With that, Rosemary turned to her son and asked, "Would you like that, Ben?" His answer, "Oh, yes," came in an instant. Two hours later, Rosemary had a passport and a round-trip ticket for Ben. "You can take him with you tomorrow," she said.

So Ben came to Washington for a two-week stay with us—which turned out to be a good thing for all of us. While Brenda took care of Sean, I took Ben in hand. I drove him around

Washington, showing him the Lincoln Memorial, the Jefferson Memorial, the Congress, the National Cathedral, and the White House. We visited the Air and Space Museum and the Washington Zoo. I took him to Alexandria Old Town and showed him the little house we had bought there, then went to the marina where the cabin cruiser we had sold was still moored. I also took him to see Sean's apartment.

Ben was thrilled at everything he saw. He was a bright youngster, and I enjoyed being with him. I took photographs of him everywhere we went so he could show them to his mother and friends when he returned to England.

He did not know how to swim, so every morning I gave him swimming lessons in our pool until, finally, he could swim across the pool without assistance. He was so excited about his accomplishment that he did it again and again. Before his visit was over, he could swim the length of the pool.

He played with Caesar and proved to be adept at training him. The little dachshund obeyed every command Ben gave him. I had the unfulfilled hope that Caesar would obey us in the same way after Ben returned home.

Every day, when we returned from our outings, I would take over the care of Sean so Brenda could spend time with Ben. We told him that Sean was very ill, a fact he accepted without question.

Without realizing it, our "visitor" helped take our minds off some of our problems—at least for a while. On the day we took Ben to Dulles Airport, he cried and said he didn't want to leave us—and Caesar. As a souvenir, I bought Ben an outsized plastic model of an F-16 fighter plane. Since it was too big to fit in his luggage, he carried it with him as he boarded the plane.

Beginning that last week of July and throughout August, Sean began to suffer the same symptoms as last year at this time, plus a few new ones. He lost weight and had high fevers and night sweats that soaked his pillows and sheets. His neuropathy returned, especially in his right leg, which was painful from his toes to his knee. He said his leg joints seemed to be stiffening, and he reported sharp pains in his stomach, which his doctor attributed to the aspirin he took to control his fever. He also said his stomach felt bloated all the time.

Hoping that things would improve again, I purchased tickets to the South of France. Somehow, with those in hand, we felt that everything would be all right.

Meanwhile, the transmission on Sean's car broke down for the third time in a year. Each time it was very expensive to repair. Sean paid what he could, but the costs were beyond his means. After discussing it with Brenda, I decided to turn it in for a new Honda Prelude, which we did the following day. We gave it to our son as an early Christmas present, and he was thrilled.

When Sean saw his specialist again on August 24, he weighed 138 pounds—enough to keep him out of the hospital. The doctor drew blood for a variety of tests and said he would have the results in a week. He renewed Sean's current prescriptions and added Halcion to help him sleep.

The specialist called on August 31 with the results of Sean's blood tests. His T4 count was 116. In light of this, the doctor said that Sean must start a treatment called aerosol pentamidine once a month for the rest of his life to prevent pneumocystis pneumonia. He should take the first two treatments before leaving for France. This required a compressor, which I obtained from the home nursing service. The nurse showed me how to administer the medication, which was transformed into a mist by the compressor and inhaled by Sean through a tube. We gave Sean the first treatment on September 11 and the second on the day before our departure for France. Silently, I prayed that this would fend off pneumocystis pneumonia, an opportunistic infection that was almost always fatal.

Sean's fever and chills returned on September 17. When he saw his specialist three days later, Sean weighed 143 pounds. A week before our scheduled departure, Sean's neuropathy was so painful, he could hardly put weight on his feet. He had high fevers and night sweats.

Brenda and I were concerned that the arduous trip would be too much for Sean, but he would not hear of canceling it. He insisted we go, remembering the healing effect it had on him during the last visit.

I arranged to have a wheelchair available for Sean at the airport in Washington, then in Paris, and in the South of France. Especially now, we all felt a sense of urgency about returning to the old château and its healing powers. We could not, would not, give up hope.

14

Traveling to the South of France was the most difficult part of our vacation. After rushing to get to the airport on time, we had to wait interminably before we could board the plane. Then we had the monotonous flight across the Atlantic, only to rush in Paris to catch the shuttle bus to another airport for the connecting flight to the South of France. This left us all exhausted. But it was particularly trying for Sean.

It was only when we settled into our rented car for the drive to the château that we could appreciate the balmy air and the beautiful blue of the Mediterranean. Sean eased back in the car and seemed to savor the surroundings. When we pulled up to the iron gates to the château, "Prince" was there again to greet us. He nuzzled Sean in recognition. As we crossed the courtyard and entered the château, we knew that the reward at the end more than made up for any inconvenience in getting there.

We installed Sean and Don in the downstairs suite with French doors leading out to the garden. Sean, his eyes now bright with excitement, eagerly showed Don the features of the château and the grounds.

After a simple lunch and a nap, Sean was ready to take Don down to the village. The magic of this wonderful place had already lifted Sean's spirits, and the debilitating ills he had suffered seemed to vanish. I couldn't believe the transformation in him; it renewed my own spirit.

Brenda and I considered ourselves fortunate to have been able to bring Sean here in February and again this time with his friend Don, so that he could share the memories we had always treasured from our many visits here over the years.

Later, the four of us drove down to the lower village, where supermarkets had been built to accommodate the needs of thousands of vacationers who now poured in during the summer. Because this was October, the streets were relatively quiet. We shopped for provisions at the supermarket, then went down to the beach to admire the sea. It was late afternoon, and the beach was nearly empty. We discussed plans to drive to some of the other villages and towns along the Riviera during our stay.

Brenda wanted to buy some Picault dishes in Valauris to augment those we had bought years before and, on the same outing, visit Biot and St. Paul de Vence. Don, who had seen the remarkable Provençal dolls in a shop window, wanted to get one for his mother.

We thought the market in the Place des Templiers in the old part of Hyères would interest Don and Sean. There we used to buy some of the best strawberries in the world. I suggested that we might take a boat trip to the Iles d'Hyères.

Sean particularly wanted to return to Saint-Tropez, and Don was eager to see it as well. We thought we could combine that with a visit to the hilltop villages of Gassin and Ramatuelle. Other ideas would occur to us as we went along.

All these outings would be liberally interspersed with strolls through the village and countryside, swimming and sunbathing. I drove Sean and Don to the beach most afternoons—a wide, fine-sand beach among the best on the French Riviera.

In the next two weeks, we made all the excursions we planned. We climbed the steep narrow streets of the old section of Hyères, where colorful and fragrant food shops of every description lined both sides of the street. The stands in the open market in the Place des Templiers offered vegetables, flowers, and fruits.

It was Sunday when we went to Gassin and Ramatuelle. Mass had just ended in Gassin, and the parishioners flowed into the streets, where they gathered in the sun to visit with one another. As we strolled through this lovely old hilltop town, I photographed Brenda, Sean, and Don in those picturesque settings. The street that encircled the town gave us views from a dizzying height of the vineyards below. In the distance, we could see the Bay of Saint-Tropez.

We went on to Ramatuelle. Sunday was market day there. As with all French street markets, it was a spectacle. There were stands hung with swatches of colorful fabrics in Provençal patterns, now so popular in America. There were vegetable stands with piles of bright red tomatoes, green beans, melons, and peaches. There was a cheese stand and one with various kinds of ham. There was even one with fossils that had entrapped fish and flora. Milling about as they shopped were hundreds of townsfolk, dressed in their Sunday best.

From Ramatuelle, we drove down the steep winding road to Saint-Tropez. Unlike on our previous visit, the town dozed in the sunshine. There were many yachts of impressive size from various countries moored in the port, their crews busily polishing brass fittings and painting or varnishing woodwork. Casually dressed owners and their friends lounged on deck, drinks in hand.

We strolled along the quayside, shopping for T-shirts and other mementos of our visit. Don bought the Provençal doll he wanted for his mother. Then we went on to the Old Port where work-oriented fishing boats were pulled up onto the beach.

Tired from all our walking during the morning, we settled into the comfortable red canvas chairs at Senéquier's and ordered drinks. Here we introduced Don to *pastis*, a strong, re-freshing, licorice-flavored regional drink so popular in the South of France.

Saint-Tropez had always been one of our favorite towns. When Brenda and I first visited it in 1949, it was a placid place, with pastel-colored houses that overlooked the port and bay. (It had not yet been discovered by Brigitte Bardot and her fol-lowers, who swarmed into the town by the thousands during the summer season, jamming the streets and cafés.) As the four of us sat in Senéquier's enjoying our drinks on that sunny Octo-ber day, Saint-Tropez seemed to be much as it was in 1949. Sean's first grim impression of it five months ago, when we were buffeted by that mighty storm, was now dimmed as he saw it as we had described it to him years ago.

From the very first time we stayed in the château, we had frequently heard noises at night—the sound of footsteps, of a door opening or closing, the shuffling sounds of someone else in the place. They would have been inconsequential if there had been others with us there, but since Brenda and I were alone, and both of us heard them, we could only attribute them to the unique atmosphere of the castle. If they were the sounds of spirits, they were benign, and we were not troubled by them. Between ourselves, we attributed these sounds to "Gaspard," the nobleman whose tomb had been discovered sealed in a cel-lar wall when the château was being restored. The coffin was reverently removed and the remains identified as those of Jo-seph Gaspard de Covet, the twenty-second lord of the domain. The coffin was then carefully replaced and sealed back into the wall where it was found.

It was Gaspard de Covet who, in memory of the miracles of Saint François de Paul, turned the château over to the Order of

Minimes in 1664. Perhaps that explained why the château had such a healing effect on Sean.

Our return to Washington was similar to our flight to France. But when we reached our home, tired as we were, we knew that this had been an experience that Sean and Don would never forget. More important, Sean seemed strong and healthy. During our entire stay at the château, he did not experience any fever, pain, or other manifestations of his disease, which so plagued his life in Washington. His blond hair, now bleached by the sun, contrasted sharply with his dark tan. He looked wonderful.

It reminded me of something I once read by a terminally ill minister: "I'm not going to die from dying. I'm going to die from living."

IV

APPROACHING
DARKNESS

15

On October 25, the day after our return from France, Sean was informed by his former employer that his group health insurance would be canceled at the end of the month. In total shock, I called him for an explanation. He said that a representative of the health-insurance company told him that because of his firm's "bad record," the group insurance rate for the entire office staff was about to increase 77 percent. He singled out Sean's case saying that his illness could potentially cost the company $250,000. So Sean's coverage, as well as that of other former employees, would be cut off effective October 31, 1989. The excuse given was that COBRA, which guaranteed health insurance coverage for eighteen months after retirement for health reasons, did not apply to firms with fewer than twenty employees.

This was an appalling, not to mention unexpected, development. I had just picked up three of Sean's medications, Zovirax, Cipro, and Retrovir (AZT), for a total cost of $664.34—which represented only a fraction of Sean's medical costs. His doctors' bills, lab tests, and hospital stays cost an astronomical amount, of which, with health insurance, we paid 20 percent.

In order to keep ahead of spiraling medical costs, we had already sold our collection of antique silver, as well as paintings, some tapestries, antique furniture, our apartment in Paris, and historic documents—including a banknote signed by Roosevelt, Churchill, and Stalin, which I had acquired at the Yalta Conference. This latest development proved to me the absolute necessity for prompt health-care reform. The COBRA loophole suggests that employees of small firms are somehow less worthy than those of large firms. If and when health reform is finally enacted, this discriminatory loophole must be eliminated.

Are only AIDS patients discriminated against by health-insurance companies, or are others affected with diseases for which there is no cure, like cancer and Alzheimer's, also obliged to shoulder a disproportionate share of medical costs? It all seems incomprehensible, not to mention unjust. On a related note, there is no doubt in my mind that pharmaceutical companies are pricing their medications far beyond the cost of developing them. While they should, of course, receive a fair return on their investment, in my view this practice has been abused, and there seems to be no procedure in place to control it.

Hospitals also are too often motivated more by profit than need, as seen by costly, painful, and often unnecessary tests and procedures inflicted on terminally ill patients who are helpless to resist.

Since Sean, because of his disability and lack of savings, now qualified for Medicaid, we sent his application in immediately. We were told, however, that it would be forty-five days before it would take effect. Knowing that in that period the cost of Sean's medications could reach dizzying heights, I urged that office to do everything in its power to expedite approval of his application. I also explored the possibility of converting Sean's group insurance coverage to individual coverage. It was much more expensive, but we had to have him covered in case he would be hospitalized.

Additionally, I looked into the possibility of restoring his coverage under my own health-insurance policy. Sean had been dropped from this coverage when he reached the age of twenty-two. But because he was diagnosed as HIV positive two months *before* his twenty-second birthday and was therefore disabled, he possibly could be reinstated. In conversations with my health insurance company, it turned out that Sean did qualify for reinstatement.

I spent the next few days collecting and submitting the necessary documents to activate both Medicaid and my health insurance coverage for Sean. The Medicaid coverage was important because it reduced the cost of prescription drugs to fifty cents apiece! In the interim, until these came on line, I succeeded in converting Sean's group coverage to individual coverage. The cost of the monthly premium rose from $92.20 to $279.70—an increase of 300 percent.

We received notification from the Department of Human Services that Sean's Medicaid "spend-down" figure was allotted to be $249.66 a month. This meant that Sean would not receive his Medicaid benefits if his monthly expenses were less than that figure. In fact, the cost of his monthly individual health insurance premium alone automatically qualified him.

These few days were hectic and emotionally charged, but fortunately Sean's coverage did not lapse.

16

In contrast to the good health Sean sustained for months following our February vacation at the château, this time his symptoms came back with a rush.

A further problem arose when, a few weeks later, I was assigned to jury duty and was selected for a narcotics case. My absence placed a very heavy burden on Brenda, who had counted on me to help care for Sean and administer his various medications.

In court, I asked permission to speak to the judge. I told him that our son was dying of AIDS and that the burden of care was more than my wife could carry alone. In response to his question, I told him we had no other relatives who could assume my share of responsibility. I requested that I be excused. When he warned this could cause a mistrial, I said that I was sorry, but I would have to insist. Reluctantly, he excused me. (I later learned from a fellow juror that there was no mistrial, and the drug dealer was found guilty.)

That Thanksgiving, we invited Don to share the holiday with us. Brenda made elaborate preparations for a traditional Thanksgiving dinner. I lit a fire in the hearth, and we enjoyed the warmth of one another's company—particularly because Thanksgiving was always one of Sean's favorite family holidays. Although he got through that day fairly well, the cycle soon after reverted.

Despite his worsening condition, Sean invited us to dinner at an Indian restaurant to celebrate Brenda's birthday on December 14; he knew that she particularly liked Indian food. But he only picked at his own dinner and ate practically nothing, telling us the spicy food played havoc with his thrush.

Earlier in December, Sean and Don had invited thirty-five friends to Sean's apartment for a pre-Christmas party on December 17. Although this seemed to me to be an ambitious undertaking, it served to help take Sean's mind off his illness for a few weeks. And Brenda and I both helped. For two days prior to the cocktail party, Brenda made enough hors d'oeuvres of various kinds for all the guests, while I made a stand for Sean's Christmas tree. He and I then together decorated the tree with lights and ornaments. Sean hung a Christmas wreath on the apartment door, and we strung colored lights on his balcony. Since Sean tired easily and frequently was breathless, he had to rest repeatedly. But we enjoyed this common effort, and I prayed that the spirit of Christmas would keep our son going.

The party was a great success. It was our first opportunity to meet so many of Sean and Don's friends. They were interesting and seemed genuinely happy to meet us, too. Sean and Don had hired a bartender and two waiters so they would be free to enjoy their company. The apartment looked beautiful, the Christmas tree and balcony lights were spectacular.

It was bitterly cold on the first day of winter. Sean had a fever and was nauseous and weak. Inexplicably, his stomach was becoming bloated. To compound things, Don was leaving the following day for California to be with his parents for Christmas. I've never seen Sean's morale so low.

On Christmas Eve, Sean confided to me he had been having a problem with the vision in his right eye for about a month. He described it as a "shadow" on the three-to-six o'clock quadrant, which interfered with his peripheral vision. He said he wanted to determine if the CMV had infected his eye. After seeking the advice of his specialist, Sean made an appointment with an ophthalmologist.

Meanwhile, the three of us went to Midnight Mass on Christmas Eve. Sean wouldn't miss that for anything. He carefully watched the altar servers as they performed their duties and was satisfied that they did well, even though he had not coached them this year.

On December 29, we heard from the ophthalmologist that Sean did *not* have CMV retinitis. While he could not determine the cause of white spots on the retina of Sean's right eye, the doctor said the spots could be caused either by tuberculosis or toxoplasmosis, for which he would have to be tested. He called Sean's specialist and urged him to order a Magnetic Resonance Imaging (MRI) and conduct a number of blood tests to help diagnose the problem.

That evening, Sean was in obvious great pain. He said his gums hurt, he was nauseous, he had stomach cramps, and his neuropathy was very painful. And I knew just how awful he must have felt when he volunteered, "I would be willing to go into the hospital for a couple of days for the blood tests and the MRI"—without any prompting from us. This change in attitude surprised us, because he had always fought the idea of going into the hospital.

Sean's spirits rose with Don's return on December 30. He slept soundly for fourteen hours straight. When he called on the thirty-first, he sounded much better. He said he had a good breakfast and told us that he and Don were going out to dinner and then to a nightclub to celebrate New Year's Eve. But the nightclub was so crowded that Sean had to stand for several hours. This aggravated his neuropathy and caused acute pain. He later told us that it felt as if he were walking on broken glass. It was so painful, in fact, that Don had to carry him up the stairs when they got home.

The owner of the château called me on January 5, 1990, to ask when we wanted to rent the château again. Still hopeful, I reserved two weeks in May beginning on the fourteenth. I told Sean about this when he had breakfast with us the next morning. He nodded in approval, but seemed vague and went to sleep right after eating. He would wake up from time to time, would say something incoherent, then go back to sleep. His respiration was very rapid. I called his physician, who suggested this could be due to Sean's fever. He advised that Sean have a chest X ray to make sure that pneumocystis pneumonia had not set in. The X ray indicated that while there were spots on Sean's lungs, they were not caused by pneumocystis pneumonia. We were relieved at this news. But his specialist still seemed to be concerned, especially since Sean had a dry cough, chest pains, and shortness of breath.

Sean began spending more and more time at our house, either coming over for breakfast or staying overnight. He was eating well again, and his spirits were high. Nevertheless, he continued to have fevers in excess of 100 degrees, his neuropathy still plagued him, and he continued to have breathing problems.

Our emotions were yanked from one extreme to another as Sean's condition worsened or improved. Such is the cycle of AIDS.

In the meantime, a popular member of our parish had died after being in a coma for two months. We went to church for the memorial service. Every pew was filled, and there was standing room at the back. The service was long, and Sean became tired and uncomfortable. When we returned home, he went right to sleep. Later, he forgot that he had even attended the memorial service. This was a frightening sign.

My worries increased when my health-insurance company began giving signals it was not going to pay for Sean's aerosol-pentamidine treatment that the specialist had prescribed to prevent pneumocystis pneumonia. The insurance company's excuse was that they did not pay for preventative medicine. This seriously concerned me because that treatment was so costly. Meanwhile, Sean's individual insurance coverage would remain in force only until February 1. Fortunately, if necessary, we could renew it for another month.

In the middle of all this, Sean tripped and fell, fracturing a bone in his right foot. The orthopedist put his leg in a half-cast, which Sean had to wear for about thirty days. The doctor prescribed a painkiller and a pair of crutches. I took Sean back to our house, where I installed him on the couch in the living room. Then we had to bring in a physical therapist to train Sean in the use of the crutches. Soon he was able to get around the house and even up and down stairs with little difficulty.

There was one positive side to this accident, however: It effectively prevented Sean from driving his car. We had been worried about that because his vision was so poor.

17

When I went to pick up various prescriptions for Sean, including sulfadiazine to correct his diminished vision, the pharmacist told me that he could not fill the whole prescription for sulfadiazine pills because these were no longer being manufactured. I took those he had on hand, which were enough for about two weeks.

When Sean called us early the next morning, his speech was so thick that I could hardly understand him. Furthermore, he was incoherent—almost delirious. This was so strange that I asked to speak to Don.

"Sean's in a bad way," Don said. "He's very unsteady on his feet, and he fell once in the house, but he didn't hurt himself. He had only two drinks last night, and he ate a good dinner, but then he threw up. All last night he tossed and turned in bed and spoke in disconnected sentences. His hands are shaking now, and his speech is slurred. I think he should be in the hospital. I'll drive him straight over to your house this morning."

All this sounded to me as if Sean had taken an overdose of sulfadiazine, which, combined with the two drinks he had, might be the root of the problem. Each time Sean took sulfadiazine, he became confused.

Don and Sean arrived home an hour later. Sean was shaking, delirious, and could barely stand. Somehow, half-carrying him,

Don and I got him up the front steps and onto the couch in the living room. I called the ophthalmologist and described the situation. He recommended that I stop giving Sean sulfadiazine. In the meantime, Sean fell sound asleep, but his respiration was rapid. He slept all day. When he woke up at ten o'clock that night, he was lucid. He must have been very hungry, because he asked for a roast-beef sandwich—and ate it. Then, Don and I managed to get Sean upstairs to bed in his room, where he fell back to sleep immediately.

Don was a great help to us during these times. I don't know how we could have gotten through this latest ordeal without him. He stayed overnight at our home, sleeping on the couch.

At four o'clock in the morning, I heard a crash from Sean's room. When I investigated, I found he had fallen against the portable commode next to his bed. He said he had tried to get up to go downstairs for some Gatorade, apparently forgetting that I had left a full glass for him next to his bed.

Thankfully, he was not hurt, and I helped him get back into bed. Then I noticed some blood on the floor. Sean had cut his heel when he fell. Wearing surgical gloves, I sprayed the wound with Mediquik and covered it with a Band-Aid.

His mind was wandering again. As I dressed his wound, he said, "I would like to have a piece of the pizza Mother made for me." I assured him that he had only dreamed that his mother had made him a pizza. Then, inexplicably he commented, "We must rent an oxygen tent tomorrow." Next, he imagined his vision was diminishing because he was no longer taking sulfadiazine. The thought of going blind terrified him.

I talked to Sean's specialist the next day, and I described to him the crisis we had gone through. He was particularly concerned about Sean's mental state. "Sean must go to the hospital tomorrow morning." There was a sense of urgency in his voice. Worried about Sean's mental change over the past five days, the specialist ordered a CAT scan of the brain. At the hospital, a doctor drew blood for some tests and put Sean on an IV to deal with dehydration. Because Sean continued to be short of breath, had a dry cough, and was experiencing chest pains, his specialist said these symptoms could be caused by pneumocystis pneumonia and that a bronchoscopy would be performed.

Sean's hospital dinner was an unappetizing mess of chunks of meat swimming in gravy, strained collard beans, rice, a cream soup of mysterious origin, a cup of tepid water for tea, and chocolate ice cream that had melted to a soupy consistency. Disgusted, Sean refused to eat any of it.

No one had bothered to give Sean any medication after he was admitted. I complained about this to the nurse because Sean obviously had a high fever. When she took his temperature, it was 103.2 degrees. She gave him some Tylenol. Later, when the resident doctor made his rounds, I told him that it was absolutely essential that Sean have the medications prescribed for him and that I would be glad to provide them. "That's against the rules," he said. "Now that Sean is in the hospital, his medications are the hospital's responsibility."

I was furious and protested with some heat. The doctor relented and ordered some Nizoral, Mycelex, and, for Sean's neuropathy, Amitriptyline.

I was not at all impressed by this hospital. It was not our first choice, but since it was the hospital to which Sean's specialist was accredited, we had no alternative. To change hospitals would have meant to change his specialist—and that was unthinkable.

Sean was first told that the bronchoscopy would be performed only if his blood clotted in six minutes; but when the test was made, his blood took sixteen minutes to clot. The surgeon prescribed a transfusion of platelets. This reduced the clotting time to eight minutes, allowing the surgeon to perform the bronchoscopy and a bronchial wash. He promised to have the results of the biopsy in forty-eight hours.

Sean called us at two-forty the next morning to say that he had fallen trying to get to the bathroom and that a male nurse had to carry him back to his bed. He apologized for calling at this hour, but he felt he had to tell us. In frustration, I immediately called the nurses' station. They told me that Sean did *not* fall. He had used his crutches to get to the bathroom and was escorted there and back by a male nurse. I was told that Sean was a little confused. The changes in his mental condition still remained a mystery.

A day later, the specialist told us that the bronchoscopy and bronchial wash confirmed that Sean did not have pneumocystis pneumonia. The doctor went on to say that the biopsy on Sean's lung revealed a small infection that could be chlamydia. After writing a prescription for doxycycline to treat this, he released Sean from the hospital.

Before leaving, Sean complained to his specialist about the poor nursing care in the hospital. He pointed out that the nurse had released him with a catheter still in his arm. I chimed in with my own list of complaints. The doctor promised to talk to the head nurse.

After settling in back home, with our help, Sean had his first real bath in a tub since he had broken his foot. He soaked luxuriously for a half hour in the hot, sudsy water and emerged physically and mentally relaxed.

The ophthalmologist examined Sean the next day and said the "cotton wool balls" in his right eye were getting smaller. "Keep taking the Daraprim and leucovorin," he advised, "but don't take sulfadiazine, because it may have caused that dramatic allergic reaction."

When Brenda was helping Sean get up from the couch, he had a dizzy spell. Both he and Brenda fell down. On the way down, they collided with the marble-top coffee table, which collapsed. The stool next to the couch fell on top of Sean, striking him on the bridge of his nose. Both were shaken up by the accident, but fortunately, neither was seriously hurt.

Despite his fall, Sean began walking without his crutches by March 1. Since he was still unsteady on his feet, I stayed close by him or had him take my arm for support.

In the meantime, Sean was terribly upset because his eyesight was diminishing so swiftly. Desperate to save the vision in his right eye, he called his ophthalmologist and begged to be allowed to take sulfadiazine again. The doctor relented, saying that Sean could take just one at noon, and if there was no allergic reaction, he could resume the normal dosage in the evening. Sean followed his instructions. Three hours after taking the first pill, he experienced severe reactions: a hot flush, dizziness, thickened speech, and rapid respiration. By 5:00 p.m., his temperature rose. His nasal passages blocked up, forcing him to breathe through his mouth. By four-thirty the following morning, he had a fever of 104.1 degrees, and his speech was incoherent.

These alarming symptoms, which began soon after he took the sulfadiazine, were identical to those that prompted his specialist to put him into the hospital on January 8. I was convinced that Sean had a violent allergy to sulfadiazine, an opinion shared by the ophthalmologist, who ordered Sean to throw away the remaining sulfadiazine tablets. I'd had no idea that an allergy from a medication could actually be life-threatening, my previous exposure to allergies being limited to sneezing or a rash from hay fever. Sometimes, the cure is worse than the illness. And so I made sure Sean would never take this medication again.

The ophthalmologist finally identified the white spots, or lesions, on Sean's eyes as toxoplasmosis. He said he had never before seen toxoplasmosis lesions as big as those on Sean's right eye. Their size was what prevented him from making his diagnosis sooner. Sean's uncorrected vision in his right eye was 20/800 (20/20 being normal). With his left eye covered, Sean could not detect the number of fingers held up just three feet in front of him, meaning that he was virtually blind in his right eye.

In mid-March, X rays showed that Sean's lung was completely clear of all chlamydia infection, so there was no need to renew the prescription for doxycycline.

At last, something seemed to be working.

18

Suddenly, on March 22, Brenda decided she must visit her mother in England to be with her on her ninety-fifth birthday. She felt impelled to go. At the same time, she didn't want to leave Sean at this critical stage of his illness. I assured her that I could take care of him with the help of his doctors, his nurse, and Don. I pointed out that Doris had no one but Brenda to look after her. With this encouragement, Brenda asked me to book her passage on April 23 so that she would arrive on the morning of her mother's birthday for a one-week stay. She telephoned her cousin Rosemary in the North of England to request that she meet her at Manchester Airport with a birthday cake and a bouquet of flowers for Doris, for which Brenda would reimburse her.

A week after I booked Brenda's airline ticket, she received a letter from her mother pleading that she spend a week with Doris in time for her ninety-fifth birthday. Doris's letter was postmarked March 22, the very day Brenda felt the strong urge to go to England. Here was yet another manifestation of Brenda's "gift."

On Sean's insistence, we attended the Easter Vigil at our parish. This was always Sean's preference; and we could not dissuade him, despite the fact he tired quickly, and we knew it would be difficult and exhausting—which indeed it was. He returned home in a weakened condition and went right to bed.

Sean could no longer fit into any of his trousers because of his bloated stomach. This meant his large wardrobe of Italian clothes was virtually useless. So, as an Easter present, Brenda took him shopping for some trousers that fit.

On the eve of her trip to England, Brenda made a batch of French pancake batter, a couscous salad, and a pasta salad for Sean and me so we could have plenty of good things to eat while she was away. I took her to the airport for her flight.

Meanwhile, Sean was determined to build up his strength. He joined me one morning when I took Caesar out for a walk, and then he started walking with us every day. He would exercise with weights at home, after which he and I would go to the exercise room in his building and work out for twenty minutes. Sean used the weight machines, the exercycle, and the rowing machine. I, less energetic than he, confined myself to the treadmill and the exercycle. But Sean could keep this up for only a few days.

At this time, I noticed that Sean's short-term memory seemed to be impaired. He knew something was wrong, too. He still couldn't recall attending the funeral service, or the sessions with the physical therapist who had trained him to use his crutches. He told his specialist that he feared the Halcion prescribed for sleep was affecting his memory so the doctor replaced Halcion with Benadryl. Still, Sean was preoccupied with worry and disappointment. He was concerned that his health had not improved as much as he anticipated. "I don't think I'll be able to climb the spiral stairway to the ramparts, and I may not be able to make it up that steep path to the château," he confessed. I thought of canceling our planned trip to France in May.

～

Brenda called us three days after she arrived in England. She was obviously upset and dismayed at what she found. She said that when she and Rosemary arrived at the house, her mother hugged Rosemary, but she didn't recognize Brenda, asking, "And who is this lady?" Brenda was devastated. (Eventually, Doris realized that "this lady" was indeed her daughter, Brenda, who had arrived from America for her birthday, just as she said she would.)

"The situation in Mother's house is dreadful," Brenda went on. "She's still as frugal as she ever was. When I turned on the electric water heater so I could take a hot bath, Mother switched it off, saying it would cost too much in electricity. Whenever she leaves the house, she turns off the main electric switch, so when she returns, the refrigerator is warm."

Everything was obviously out of control. Brenda added that Doris fell down all the time, that she put water in the kettle on the stove for tea, and then would forget about it. She had burned out three kettles this way, and Brenda feared the house might burn down one day unless something were done. Also, she would sometimes turn on the gas and forget to light it. The biggest worry was that, were she to have an accident when her neighbors were out, there would be no one to help her.

Further, Brenda reported that her mother bedeviled all the neighbors. She always walked into the house next door without knocking, to her neighbors' extreme annoyance. When Brenda suggested she at least knock first and wait to be let in, Doris replied, "But they're always happy to see me."

Brenda took Doris for an outing in her wheelchair, pushing her in the street to avoid the curbs, as there was no wheelchair access to the sidewalks. Her mother gesticulated wildly with her cane as she pointed out the houses of her neighbors. This rattled oncoming drivers, who panicked and swerved to avoid being hit by the cane.

Brenda related that when her mother complained she couldn't sleep at night, she gave her a sleeping pill. Her mother talked in her sleep all night long and was hallucinating in the morning. Only then did Brenda discover, to her horror, that Doris had gone into her purse and taken *all* the pills, leaving the bottle empty. When Brenda told Doris's social worker what happened, the social worker insisted that Doris be put in a retirement home, but in order to qualify, she would first have to sell her house. Knowing how stubborn Brenda's mother could be, the social worker asked for Brenda's help in persuading Doris. The social worker told Brenda there was a vacancy in the nursing home that her mother had visited the previous year, and that she should take advantage of this, because vacancies are rare. Brenda went with her to see it.

She told us the retirement home had been a private estate. It had lovely gardens, comfortable accommodations, and caring personnel. The social worker told Brenda it was the very best in the North of England. So Brenda made the necessary arrangements to have Doris admitted. She planned to check with a real estate agent about selling her mother's house. "I can't wait to leave here and come home again," she said.

Sean and I were distressed at the problems Brenda had encountered and sorry she had to face them alone—especially since she was already burdened with her concern for Sean.

Three days later, Brenda called again while I was out taking Caesar for a walk. Sean asked her, "On a scale of one to ten, how is your visit going with Granny?" "Less than two," Brenda replied. She told him about putting the house up for sale and that she had given the real estate agent power of attorney, which she could do because she owned the house jointly with her mother. She said her mother would be moving into the retirement home at the end of the week.

Brenda told us she helped her mother sort out what she would take with her to the home and what she would leave. Every time Brenda put something in the discard pile, her mother would take it back. Finally, Brenda thought they had it worked out. They agreed that whatever was left would be given to charity.

Brenda left the next day for home; but as she was about to set out for the airport, Doris announced that she had decided not to go into the retirement home, and that she was going to keep her house and everything in it.

Brenda looked at her in disbelief as she rode off. As frustrating as this was, Brenda felt that she had laid the groundwork for her mother's well-being. She had arranged for her to enter the retirement home, she had organized the selling of her house and the disposal of her furnishings.

Later, we learned that while Brenda was still on her way back to America, her mother relented and decided to enter the retirement home after all. She remained there until she died shortly before her ninety-ninth birthday.

19

Sean, Caesar, and I were at the airport to greet Brenda. It was both a relief and a joy to have her back. She was shocked to see how much Sean's condition had deteriorated in the week she was away. We stood in a long embrace while Caesar jumped up and down with excitement.

By now Sean had great difficulty walking. He was terribly tired after walking just one short block and back with Caesar and me. The steps up to the front door were particularly arduous for him. Recognizing his limitations, he now took my arm as a matter of course when he walked anywhere.

On May 5, as we drove Sean to Don's house, he told us how fearful he was about making the trip to France. "When the trip was a month away," he said, "I was sure my health would improve. Now we're leaving in a week, and my health is still rotten."

Brenda spoke sternly to Sean. "You have to fight to survive. You must eat. You must stop smoking. It cuts your appetite and contributes to your shortness of breath. If you won't help yourself, I can't help you."

Sean was subdued, unsure of himself, which was extremely uncharacteristic of him.

The next day, he seemed better. He sunbathed for an hour. And he cut back on the cigarettes, smoking just seven all day.

He *looked* well. Nonetheless, I privately worried that the strain of the trip to France would take its toll. Then I convinced myself that once he was in the château, Sean would be all right.

On the Saturday morning prior to our scheduled flight, I took Caesar to the shuttle, which picked him up and took him to the kennels where he would stay while we were away. I felt a twinge in my heart as I left him there. He was a part of our family—and a real "tonic" for Sean.

That evening, Sean and Don attended an AIDS benefit dinner, where, Sean said, he ate very well.

After Mass on Sunday, May 13, we made final preparations for our departure that evening. I made certain that a wheelchair would be waiting for Sean at Dulles Airport and at the gate of Charles de Gaulle Airport.

Sean was not able to do much during our stay at the château from May 14 to May 29. His neuropathy was so painful that he could walk only about twenty yards before he had to sit down and rest. So he would not have to use the stairs to the downstairs suite, we gave the master bedroom on the main floor to him and Don. Walking down to the village was out of the question for him, so he and Don sunbathed in the courtyard. As he predicted, he was not able to climb the stairs to the ramparts. "Prince," his "dog away from home," was his constant companion and a great comfort to him.

We ate well at the château, and Sean's appetite was hearty. For breakfast we had croissants, often still warm from the oven, with sweet butter and jam. Brenda made delicious but simple Provençal meals for us, like *pistou*, a packaged Provençal fish soup unavailable in the United States; *pan bagnat*, a vegetable salad sandwiched between halves of a bun baked especially for this dish; and *céleri rémoulade*, a salad made of slivers of celery root in a dressing of herbs, garlic, oil, and lemon juice.

In the evenings, we played Trivial Pursuit, a game that the

owner had thoughtfully left there. Sean excelled at this, and it was good to see him in his old "competitive" mode. His mind was again as sharp as it had always been.

Since my birthday came during our trip, Don took us all out to dinner at one of the village cafés. We sat on the terrace with a view overlooking the sea and out onto the square. Here we watched the villagers relax after a long day in the fields. There, for an hour or so, it was as if time were suspended and the anguish we all had endured had faded in the lowering light.

On one occasion, I drove Don and Sean down to the beach. I was able to park close enough that Sean did not have to walk too far on the sand. He wanted only to sunbathe; he did not attempt to swim. I was heartsick to see his once-strong, lithe body now wasting away. His eyes were sunken, and his hair was becoming thin. *Where is my son?* I thought. *Where are the miracles we witnessed during previous visits here?*

We made several car trips to keep Sean diverted. We rode to Saint-Tropez, where we had a drink at Senéquier's and did a little shopping. We visited La Verne Monastery, but once we reached that remote place, it was evident that Sean could not go through the ancient rambling building. Finally, we made an excursion to Aix-en-Provence because we wanted Sean to see that lovely town. Once there, I realized that Sean's vision had diminished so much that he could barely see. After lunch, we started back, but I lost my way, and it took us an inordinate amount of time to get back to the château. I should never have attempted that long a drive. It was just too much for Sean.

Unlike the first vacation at the château, and to some extent the second, this trip did not help improve Sean's physical condition. But it was relaxing for him, and a good change from the Washington environment where he seemed to spend most of his time in doctors' offices or in the hospital. Perhaps this interlude helped prepare him for the challenges he would still face.

20

Hardly a week had passed since our return from France when Sean suffered another setback. According to his ophthalmologist, CMV had infected Sean's left eye, the one in which his vision had been relatively good. With his right eye covered, Sean could not even read the big "E" on the ophthalmologist's chart. Sean acknowledged to the doctor that he could no longer see images on the TV screen and could identify actors only from their voices. He admitted that it would be impossible for him ever to drive his beautiful car again. This saddened him the most.

The ophthalmologist recommended that Sean immediately start taking ganciclovir, which could be administered by the nursing service. At home, Cathy taught me how to administer the drug by an IV. She was so competent, compassionate, and caring, I asked the nursing service to assign her to Sean as his primary nurse.

In addition, the ophthalmologist urged Sean to see a neurologist and have an MRI done of his brain to show if toxoplasmosis or CMV had infected the brain. We wasted no time. An MRI was done the next day. After his reading, the neurologist called and told me that the "white matter" in the frontal part of the brain had wasted away to a substantial degree. "This destruction of brain cells was caused by HIV infection of the brain," he explained. "This condition is responsible for Sean's headaches, lack of balance, trembling limbs, speech problems, loss of short-term memory, bloating, and loss of digestive control." Then, after a brief pause, words that hit like a thunderbolt: "It's irreversible."

I asked him for his prognosis. "A matter of months," he said.

We told Sean that HIV had invaded his brain, causing some damage, but we did not mention the neurologist's prognosis. We didn't have to. Sean knew what this meant. No doubt this prayer from his breviary was now invoked many times:

> *O Most Holy Apostle, St. Jude, faithful servant*
> *and friend of Jesus, who bears the name of the traitor*
> *who delivered thy beloved Master into the hands of his*
> *enemies and has caused thee to be forgotten by many,*
> *but the Church honors thee universally as the patron of*
> *hopeless causes and of things despaired of. Pray for me*
> *who am so miserable; make us to implore thee of thy*
> *powerful privilege accorded thee of being visible and*
> *speedy help where help is most despaired of.*

Later, when Sean stood up, he suddenly reeled and fell back on the couch where Brenda was sitting. Panic-stricken, he screamed as he fell. Brenda held him in her arms to calm him. Then, after we helped him to get upstairs, he asked his mother to come into bed with him for a while. She cradled him in her arms until he fell asleep, comforting him as only a mother can.

Our pastor, Monsignor Benson, came over for dinner on June 15, and gave Sean the blessing of the sick.

Sean endeavored to keep up a normal pace despite the terrible manifestations of his illness. He accepted each new day as a gift.

For Father's Day, Sean bought me a jar of red caviar, which

Brenda made up into a delicious spread with cream cheese and herbs and served with crackers. As Sean put the spread on his crackers, I noticed that his hands trembled. Such severe side effects were now inevitable—and unalterable. Sean was on seven different medications, taken several times a day. While these were all strong drugs, neither alone nor in combination did they constitute a cure. Even the often painful hospital interventions, for a spinal tap or a bone-marrow tap, served only to aid the doctors in diagnosing a condition and prescribing drug treatment. But such attempts were futile against the relentless advance of AIDS.

⤨

I wrote a letter to President Bush deploring his decision to cancel his scheduled address at the opening of the International AIDS Conference in San Francisco in order to attend a fund-raiser for Senator Jesse Helms, who waged a one-man war against homosexuals. I had hoped that by President Bush's appearance at the AIDS conference, he would at last publicly express his recognition of the gravity of the AIDS crisis and his determination to join in the effort of researchers and physicians to bring it to an end.

Not surprisingly, the president did not reply to my letter.

There was another frustration, too. I had applied for a handicapped parking permit for Sean in mid-June, but because of mishandling by the municipal government, we did not receive it until September.

We discussed with Sean the idea of having a permanent Groshong catheter surgically implanted in his chest. This would eliminate repeated and painful changes of temporary catheters. The Groshong could be used for all intravenous work, including the infusion of medications and fluids to counteract dehydration, withdrawing blood samples, and blood transfusions.

But Sean, who still hoped he would be able to go to the beach during the summer and sunbathe, did not want tubes protruding from his chest.

"I'll have to think about that" is all he said.

21

Sean resumed smoking heavily when we returned from France, and said defiantly he did not intend to stop. By now, his eyesight was so poor that he could no longer see the ashtray and missed it more often than not. He had already burned holes in his pajamas and bedclothes. I gave him an extra large ashtray to reduce the chance he would set the house on fire.

He told me he had just a "sliver" of vision in his left eye, which I promptly reported to the ophthalmologist. "There's nothing more I can do to save the vision in that eye," the doctor said sadly. "But Sean must continue to take ganciclovir twice a day to keep the CMV from infecting the other eye."

At Sean's next appointment, his ophthalmologist confirmed that he had lost his eyesight completely in his left eye—only thirty-four days after CMV was first detected there. He adjusted Sean's medication accordingly, to keep CMV from invading the other eye and his brain. Preoccupied with the fear of going completely blind, Sean asked the doctor if he could get an eye transplant. He said his mother offered him one of her eyes if the operation were possible. "An eye transplant is out of the question because it's impossible to suture the one million, two hundred thousand optic fibers to the optical nerve."

Sean realized then that there was no way to save his rapidly fading eyesight.

He wrote a letter in Spanish to his godparents in Argentina thanking them for a check they sent him for his birthday. His handwriting was almost illegible because of his near-blindness. Brenda had to guide his hand to keep the pen on the paper. By way of explanation, I also wrote to them and described Sean's deteriorating physical and mental condition.

His birthday was approaching. He would be twenty-six years old on July 23. Instead of celebrating it quietly ourselves, we suggested to Sean that he invite his friends to our home for a birthday party. Sean liked that idea. He drew up a list of friends and asked Don to do the inviting on his behalf. We decided to make it as festive an occasion as we could. Brenda began planning her menu.

The day of Sean's birthday party, we decorated the house. We attached a HAPPY BIRTHDAY banner to the mantelpiece, hung festoons of colored-paper streamers, and inflated dozens of balloons, using the aerosol-pentamidine compressor to inflate them. We picked up finger rolls for hors d'oeuvres and a rich chocolate cake from the pastry shop. It was a beautiful sunny day. The flowers in our garden were in full bloom.

Don and Karl, Chuck and John, Art and Mary Elizabeth, Fred and Joe, came to the party. As they arrived, they hugged Sean and offered him their gifts.

Brenda and I had talked to Art on the telephone on several occasions before, but this was the first time we met him in person. He called Sean frequently, and if Sean were asleep or in the process of being treated by Cathy, he would talk to one of us.

Art had AIDS. He was eager to talk to us because we were at Sean's side when Sean experienced some of the same crises that he endured. His friend and neighbor, Mary Elizabeth, took care of him. He said that his parents could not deal with the fact that he was gay. I saw the anguish in his eyes as he spoke. He told me he took comfort in talking to someone who was sympathetic and who understood his pain.

Karl worked in a bank. He was a handsome man with a blond mustache. He was HIV positive. He told me his parents had died, but he was close to one of his sisters and her three daughters.

Fred worked for an association of homebuilders and Joe was a lawyer.

Chuck, also a lawyer, was active on Capitol Hill as a lobbyist. In his spare time, he worked as a volunteer at the Whitman-Walker Clinic, serving as a "buddy" to men afflicted with AIDS. He brought them food, helped them file health-insurance claims, and gave them legal advice. He told me that if Sean ever needed legal help, we should turn to him.

Chuck told us that he and John had been together for ten years. When they arrived, John immediately went to the kitchen to help Brenda with the hors d'oeuvres. With real artistry, he arranged them on platters and helped serve them.

Out by the pool, we served kir royales, a champagne drink with raspberry liqueur. We also served soft drinks to those whose medications were incompatible with alcohol. Brenda passed the hors d'oeuvres, while Caesar, who loved parties, frolicked among the guests, stealing whatever food he could.

We moved inside for dinner, after which our guests showed interest in the photographs I took at the wartime conferences at Casablanca, Cairo, Teheran, and Yalta. They seemed fascinated that I knew President Roosevelt, Prime Minister Churchill, and General Eisenhower, and that I had talked personally with Joseph Stalin. They were of a different generation and knew these personalities only from their history books in high school and college.

Brenda's beauty and her ability to put guests at ease enchanted them. They admired her wit and were touched by her compassion.

It was a lively party with animated conversation. Sean looked drawn and ill, but he obviously enjoyed having his friends around him on his birthday, even though he was unable to eat anything, including his birthday cake.

We all slept soundly that night. I got up at seven-thirty to prepare Sean's ganciclovir, while Brenda, Sean, and Caesar slept on.

Don invited Sean to dinner in Alexandria. When they returned, Sean said his lack of balance was worse than it had ever been, and, indeed, I had to catch him to keep him from falling when he entered the house. This prompted us to have an iron railing installed up the front steps so Sean would have something solid to hold on to.

A few days later, in spite of his condition, Sean decided to go with Don to a party at a friend's house in Lynchburg, Virginia, and they regretted it. They returned the following afternoon after an exhausting three-and-a-half-hour drive each way. "When we arrived at the party," Sean explained, "it was crowded, and there was no place to sit down. We didn't know anyone there. My neuropathy was killing me. I ate two crackers, and then we left. I felt sick on the trip to Lynchburg, at the party, at the hotel where we stayed, and all the way home." He had eaten nothing but those two crackers from the time he left on Saturday afternoon until he returned on Sunday evening.

I made Sean a chocolate whip, and Don left after dinner. Sean, Brenda, and I, with Caesar at our side, all got into our big bed and watched television for an hour. Together we prayed before going to sleep:

> *Angel of God, my guardian dear,*
> *To whom God's love commits me here,*
> *Ever this night be at my side,*
> *To light and guard, to rule and guide.*

Karl invited Sean and Don to an outdoor evening rock concert at the Merriwether Post Pavillion on August 5. Brenda and
I seriously questioned the wisdom of this. We had visions of
Sean trying to cope with the crowds at a rock concert, being
obliged to sit on the grass for three hours, and walking from
and to the parking lot in the dark. It was an image too terrible
to contemplate.

With some prodding from us, and a firm veto from Don,
Sean was persuaded it would not be wise to go. He was pleased
that someone else had actually made the decision for him. As it
happened, it rained heavily during the concert, which would
have made the evening a certain disaster for our son.

V

SEAN'S LEGACY

22

On August 8, we went to a healing Mass at St. Peter's Catholic Church in Olney, Maryland, conducted by Father John Lubey, who was renowned for having the gift of healing. The large church was filled to capacity.

Many people there, all strangers to us, showed their concern for Sean, who they could see was very ill. One woman gave him a rosary; another, a prayer card. Others came over to us and told Sean they would pray for him. Sean was too weak to go up for the anointing. In the prayer of the faithful, there was a special prayer for people with AIDS.

The long drive to the church and back, combined with the lengthy Mass, were almost too much for Sean. He was weak and weary when we got home. When I embraced him to say good-night, I could feel all his ribs. I commented on how thin he was, and he said, "Sitting on that hard pew at St. Peter's was uncomfortable because I no longer have much padding on my buttocks."

It was urgent that he put on weight, but he couldn't digest solid food. To avoid the nausea it caused, Sean tried drinking one can of Ensure-Plus three times a day for nourishment. He couldn't keep it down. This meant that he not only lost the food value of that nourishing drink but also the medications he had taken throughout the day. On August 9, Sean's blood count was down. His specialist instructed the nursing service to give him a blood transfusion. Furthermore, the specialist decided that Sean must be fed intravenously to bypass his digestive system and get the nourishment he required. He gave full instructions to the nursing service.

So now it appeared that Sean would have to be fed intravenously for an indefinite time. He had long ago told me that he did not want to be kept alive artificially, but I couldn't bear to see him becoming thinner and weaker each day.

Cathy, Sean's home-care nurse, described the process of providing nourishment through a peripheral catheter. As she set up the IV, she explained that it would be linked to a computer-controlled electronic pump that automatically monitors the flow of nourishment into the bloodstream. It usually takes eight to ten hours to empty the Total Parenteral Nutrition (TPN) nourishment bag, so most patients prefer to have it administered at night. "If Sean ever decides to go away for a weekend," Cathy said, "he should check with his specialist to ask if he can suspend the IV feeding and get his nourishment from Ensure-Plus."

I stayed downstairs all night to be near Sean in case there were any problems with the pump. When Cathy arrived the next morning, she determined that the catheter installed the previous evening was blocked. She installed another and used it for Sean's blood transfusion.

All of Sean's resistance to a central catheter in his chest disappeared in light of the pain associated with these repeated replacements of catheters in his arms. He agreed to have the operation to implant a permanent Groshong catheter in his chest near his heart. His specialist made arrangements for this surgery.

I took Sean to Mass on August 15, the feast of the Assumption of Mary. Afterward, a score of parishioners came to our pew to greet him. Because he could no longer see their faces, they had to identify themselves to him, and I had to guide his hand to theirs. I could see they were shocked and dismayed by his appearance. I was touched by their concern, but Sean was uncomfortable at having them see him in this condition. He had always taken such pride in his appearance.

Sean desperately wanted to regain some semblance of a normal life. He was determined to go to Rehoboth Beach in Delware with Don for three days in September. I reserved a hotel room for him, but I had grave misgivings about this, particularly in view of his surgery scheduled for August 22.

I took Sean to the hospital for his catheter surgery, and he was operated on two hours later. The operation was a success. Sean stayed in the recovery room for an hour and a half and then was wheeled to his room. I stayed with him to make sure he was comfortable, then returned home for some much-needed sleep.

23

When I visited Sean in the hospital at noon the next day, he was desperate for a cigarette and was prepared to go outside the entrance of the hospital to smoke one. He gave up when he realized he was attached to the IV.

The following day, he had blood drawn through the new Groshong catheter. The process was painless, for a change. To relieve his tedium, we bought him a Walkman AM/FM stereo tape player, along with some of his favorite audiotapes.

During his visit the next day, Don called us from the hospital to say that Sean was disoriented. (Sean told him he had gone over to our house after breakfast and washed his car.) So I reported to Sean's specialist that his mind was wandering again. "When the reserve brain tissue is destroyed, as in Sean's case," he said, "mental malfunctions become increasingly evident."

When the specialist released Sean from the hospital, I told him, "I don't want to put Sean through another hospitalization. I want him to remain at home and be given whatever will make him comfortable." But the doctor warned, "In another couple of months, Sean will come down with an opportunistic disease such as pneumocystis pneumonia, accompanied by a bad cough." In spite of this, the specialist concurred and said he would abide by my wishes.

I told him that Sean was eager to go to the beach with his

friend. He gave his permission, provided Sean take the TPN nourishment for twelve hours daily. This, of course, would mean taking with him the IV pole, the electronic pump, and the bags of TPN under refrigeration. The doctor vetoed the idea of substituting Ensure-Plus. A saddened Sean pronounced that going to the beach under those conditions was "out of the question."

Still determined to live as full a life as he could, Sean told me that he and Don planned to go to an upcoming black-tie AIDS fund-raiser on Saturday, October 6. I checked with the head nurse at the nursing service to ask if I could delay Sean's TPN that night so he could attend the affair. She said I could delay it until 10:00 p.m., or even later, provided he reverted to the 7:00 p.m. schedule the following day.

At about the same time, Brenda and I received an invitation from Georgetown University to attend the President's Dinner, also being held on October 6. I accepted because I knew that Sean and Don had plans to go to the AIDS fund-raiser that night. If Sean felt ill, I knew that he was in good hands with Don and that Don would know where to reach us in case of emergency.

Sean continued to be disoriented from time to time. His long-term memory was intact; but it was his short-term memory that played tricks on him. He was confused. He thought we were going to the South of France. He had been getting his facts all mixed up. At one point, he told me he didn't feel like going out with his girlfriend in the evening. He asked repeatedly what day it was. The doctor explained that his confusion was a manifestation of advancing dementia.

Don, Chuck, and John came over to visit Sean and stayed for an hour and a half, talking and joking. These visits with Sean did wonders for his morale and gave Brenda and me a welcome respite. They borrowed a wheelchair for him from Whitman-Walker Clinic. After one of their visits, we took Sean to a shopping mall. He was pleased to get out of the house and "window-shop" from the wheelchair, although he could not see what was displayed in the windows. It was a short outing, as he tired quickly.

Things seemed to be progressively worsening. I found myself profoundly depressed by Sean's condition. His brilliant mind had deteriorated into confusion, forgetfulness, and flights of fantasy. His body had likewise deteriorated. He could walk no more than thirty feet or so, and that with great difficulty, pain, and lack of balance. He was totally blind in his left eye, and his vision in his right eye was severely impaired. Unable to retain food by mouth, he was anchored in place by the twelve-hour TPN IV feeding every day.

Our son, however, continued to fight.

On September 10, Cathy drew Sean's blood for blood-matching and took vital signs. His weight was 118 pounds. The next day, she gave him a six-hour blood transfusion.

On Sunday, as Brenda and I were preparing to go to Mass, Sean turned to me and said, "If you see my parents at Mass, tell them I don't feel well enough to go to church today." We were stunned that Sean did not recognize us. Brenda wept all through Mass. Sean's confusion lasted throughout the day. Our pastor came over that afternoon and gave him Communion and the Sacrament of the Sick.

In light of Sean's deteriorating condition, it was time to bring the double bed from the guest room down into the living room in place of the couch Sean had been using. My bad knee prevented me from helping, and the task fell to Brenda and Don. With the double bed in the living room, Sean would no longer have to climb the stairs, a difficult ordeal for him, and one of us could sleep next to him to comfort and reassure him.

Brenda's favorite cousin, Robert, called from California to ask about Sean. Brenda briefed him on Sean's current physical and mental condition. Robert expressed his sympathy for what we were all going through. He said he and his wife would be in Washington in early October to attend a wedding and would like to stop by and see us. Brenda welcomed the idea. Sean, who hadn't seen them for many years, looked forward to their visit.

Sean slept most of the following day. But he awoke disoriented, saying, "I have to call the office to tell them I won't be in for a few days." He had forgotten that he'd stopped working there two years before. Then Don and Karl dropped in and chatted with Sean for an hour or so. He enjoyed the visit, but almost immediately after they left, he forgot that they had been there.

Toward the end of September, Brenda and I took Sean to his appointment with his specialist. Sean was unsteady on his feet, even with both of us supporting him. When the doctor saw how bad the situation had become, he said he would come to our home to see Sean in the future. The ophthalmologist said the same.

We asked Don to come for dinner on September 28 and stay overnight, then and whenever he could. It meant everything to Sean to have Don near him, and we had come to consider Don a part of our family.

Brenda and I sat one evening to try to focus our thoughts. We were concerned that we might be keeping Sean alive artificially, contrary to his express wishes. An attack of Pneumocystis pneumonia would inflict terrible suffering on him. We knew none of the medications he was taking would restore his eyesight or repair the damage to his central nervous system. We discussed not only our fears but also Sean's fears, and how we could most benefit him.

Then we discussed with his physician the possibility of letting nature take its course. I suggested we eliminate all medications except those that kept Sean comfortable and pain free. He said he would support our decision.

I had to ask myself if I had been right at the outset in agreeing to put Sean on intravenous feeding—in essence, a life-support system—and now whether I should authorize removing that system, which would lead to Sean's demise. When Sean initially told me he did not want to be kept alive with tubes and machines, I readily understood and agreed with him. But when the choices were presented to me, I found myself in a quandary, knowing that whichever path I chose, I would be contributing to the death of our only child.

Brenda's cousin Robert and his wife, Helen, arrived to see us on October 2 for a luncheon visit. It was a pleasant visit as Brenda and her cousin talked about their travels and the days when they were together in London. They chatted with Sean, and he responded with full attention. Five minutes after they departed, though, Sean turned to his mother and asked, "When is your cousin coming to see us?" And at another point, when Brenda came into the room, he asked her, "Where are my parents?"

Early Saturday morning, the day we were due to go to Georgetown University's President's Dinner, Brenda was suddenly awakened by a voice that said, "Don't go, Brenda. Don't go!" The voice kept repeating, "Don't go, Brenda," all morning as she dressed and prepared breakfast. Finally, at eleven o'clock, Brenda told me, "I'm not going to the dinner tonight. You go if you like, but I'm not going." With that, the voice stopped. I knew better than to dispute her decision.

I sat down on the bed next to Sean and told him how much I loved him. And he said, "My whole life revolves around Mother and you. You both have kept me alive. Without you, I would have died long ago."

I took a slim book from the bookshelf and read to him as I

had done when he was a boy. The book was *Forever*, by Mildred Cram, a comforting story about the eternity of the soul. Sean listened with his head on my shoulder and thanked me when I finished it. Then he went to sleep.

When Don came over, he told us that because Sean was so weak and was linked to an IV for medications, transfusions, and nourishment most of the day and night, they had given up the idea of going to the AIDS fund-raiser. Don pointed out that it would be crowded, and there would be a lot of standing around before dinner. Sean agreed, and Brenda said that she had already decided not to go to the Georgetown University dinner. I opted to go to the dinner because the host had made a particular point of my attending. Also, I knew that Sean would be in good hands with both Don and Brenda with him. Brenda told Don she would make a special dinner for him.

The nurse arrived after lunch and gave Sean a two-unit blood transfusion, which would take six hours. With her in attendance, Brenda and I were able to slip out to shop for Don's dinner.

Brenda fixed dinner for Don while I put on my tuxedo and prepared to leave for the Georgetown University dinner at the Pension Building downtown. My knee was giving me a lot of pain, so Brenda suggested I take a taxi. Don arrived just as I was leaving. I greeted him and told him where I could be reached. Sean was asleep, so I did not wake him to say good-bye.

The dinner was a huge affair designed to thank those who had made substantial contributions to the university. Since I had donated my father's private papers, I was included on the guest list.

I had hardly finished the soup course when someone came to me and said he had a message for me. "Your son has had a seizure," he said. "There's a gentleman here to take you to him."

I hurried out and found Don waiting for me. As we drove

through the city, Don said, "Sean had been sleeping soundly, just as he was when you left. Then, suddenly, he began thrashing about. I couldn't restrain him. Brenda tried to reach his specialist or his regular doctor, but both were at the AIDS fundraiser that Sean and I had planned to attend. I called 911, and the emergency squad arrived as I was leaving to pick you up."

As we drove through the city, I noticed that there was a full moon. The night Sean was born, there had been a full moon just like this.

When we got back to our house, there was no one home. We learned from a neighbor that Sean had been taken to Georgetown University Hospital, and we raced over there. We found Brenda in the emergency room. Sean was lying immobile. He was dead. I went straight to him, while Brenda embraced Don. I kissed Sean and stroked his forehead. He was still warm. I told him his suffering was over at last.

Brenda picked up the account of what happened. "We were finishing dinner at about eight o'clock. Sean suddenly began thrashing about in a kind of fit. Don and I tried to control him. He had bitten his tongue, and blood trickled from the right side of his mouth. He was trying to say something to me. I caught the words 'love' and 'Mother.'

"I couldn't reach Sean's specialist or his regular doctor, but while I tried, Don, with presence of mind, raced downstairs to our tenant's apartment and called 911 for an ambulance. John [our tenant] came up and managed to get a towel between Sean's clenched teeth. I kept trying to reach Sean's specialist or his physician.

"When the emergency squad arrived, Sean's convulsions had stopped. He was very still. I'm sure he died then. But they immediately tried to revive him, while detaching him from the IV. They put him on a stretcher and carried him to the ambulance.

"Don went to fetch you, while I rode with the driver to the

hospital. En route, they continued to try to restart Sean's breathing and heartbeat. At the emergency room, the hospital staff also tried to bring him back, to no avail. At 8:55 p.m., Sean was pronounced dead. Father Curry, a Jesuit priest, gave him the last rites.

"I'm sure that Sean died at home. He told us long ago, he didn't want to die in the hospital. So we kept that promise to him."

Don drove us home, where we talked and tried to console one another. Later, Don went back to his home and Brenda and I went to bed. But sleep would not come, as the magnitude of events rushed over us.

Rather than sadness, I felt a strong sense of relief that Sean was no longer suffering. He had endured so much with silent courage. I will always be proud of him for that.

Since we couldn't sleep, we spent the night making phone calls. We called Father English, our former parish priest; my niece in California; Brenda's mother in England; my sister, Diana, in Virginia; Monsignor Benson; Sean's specialist, who, after expressing his regrets, said he would go to the hospital and sign Sean's death certificate; and Veronica, the head nurse at our nursing service.

As I paced around during the night, I noticed that my knee was pain free for the first time in months, as if Sean were now looking after me as I looked after him. I knelt and thanked God for releasing Sean from his suffering.

24

We took comfort in the knowledge that we did everything we could for Sean from the day he was born until he died. We mourned the fact that he suffered and that his life was so short, but we treasured all the time we had together and the experiences we shared. In all honesty, we could not wish him back to life as he was just before he died, and it was perhaps unrealistic to expect a miracle that would have brought him back as he was during the joyous, healthy years. The terrible vision of his illness and pain is blurred by the vivid image of all the happiness and exhilaration he brought into our lives.

Sean often carried the processional cross at religious services. As a tribute to Sean's service as sacristan and his devotion to the Church, Monsignor Benson had an oak processional cross fashioned from a pew from Our Lady of Victory Church and dedicated to Sean. A brass plaque affixed to the cross bears an inscription in his memory.

It was time for us to make adjustments to our lives. In the years before Sean was born, Brenda and I shared a full life together. We could do that again, with the added responsibility and satisfaction of helping people with AIDS and encouraging others to be compassionate toward them and their caretakers.

We started by inviting Sean's friends to dinner to express our appreciation for their visiting with him when he was so ill, lifting his spirits. They seemed to feel at ease with us, and the convivial meal helped take the pain from our hearts.

Gradually, the group expanded as Sean's friends asked if they could bring others to our home. Some who came were mourning the loss of a companion; others were isolated from their families. Some were HIV positive, some had full-blown AIDS, others were not infected but lived in fear that they might become infected. The victims of AIDS are not only those who are infected and die of the disease but also those who love them and survive.

We began having parties for the group at intervals. These were festive occasions, a time for everyone to relax and enjoy themselves. They also knew they could talk to us quietly, discussing their illness, their lost friends, and their problems. They felt "at home."

Gay men and lesbian women live in a different world behind an invisible wall of ignorance and fear that we and they have built to keep us apart. They can emerge from it—they must, to earn a living—but they come in disguise so we will not know who they are.

We sense that they are among us, but their forms are indistinct. We hear them speak, but we cannot, or will not, understand their words. We know them only by the gifts they offer us anonymously—gifts of music, of beauty, of graceful and poignant poetry.

In our presence, they are withdrawn and uncomfortable, hiding their true emotions. We recognize their remarkable abilities without really knowing much about them.

We are reticent to enter their domain, fearful of the unknown, of what we might see or hear, of being ensnared, unable to return.

Because our son was gay, he had many friends among the gay community. When he died, they rallied around us, comforted us, and, by their genuine love for Sean, gave us strength.

Gradually and gently, they guided us through the barrier into their world. It is a place full of light and laughter, of brilliant colors and subtle tones, of music, compassion, and love. Here, their form and features come into focus, and their true characters are revealed.

I have learned from them that the love gay men experience for one another is as genuine, profound, passionate, and enduring as the love between a man and a woman. Even though they are shunned by the "straight" community and deprived of religious sanctions and civil rights, their commitment to one another often lasts for decades, if not for life. The shock and sorrow if one partner dies from AIDS or any other cause is as emotionally shattering as that experienced when losing a spouse.

In their youth, with the realization that they are "different," some become withdrawn and lonely, unwilling to face the scorn and cruelty of those who do not understand them. Others try to conform to the conventional mold of masculinity, becoming adept actors at concealing their natural instincts, which, nevertheless, continue to boil up within them. The defiant ones flaunt their difference by flamboyant behavior, and in so doing, create a distorted public perception of the gay community as a whole.

The gay community is filled with people having extraordinary talents: artists, musicians, actors, designers, physicians, scientists, inventors, engineers, and statesmen. They are being struck down by AIDS as they enter their most productive years. Who knows what marvelous artistic works, what medical discoveries, what engineering miracles and peacemaking accomplishments are being blanked out by the plague of AIDS? The twenty-first century will be deprived of all these unrealized gifts.

As I write this, the group has grown to more than thirty. They are all Sean's legacy to us. We never would have met them but for our son. We have become good friends who love and support one another. We are warmed by their presence and their affection. They have become our family. Some never knew Sean but feel his presence at all these gatherings. Several have died of AIDS since Sean's passing. Doubtless, others will follow.

The AIDS plague is among us, and there is no cure or vaccine in sight. Everyone is at risk. There are no guilty or innocent victims. From the very first, those who died of AIDS were killed by the virus. A virus, by definition, is "poison," and for this HIV poison there is, as yet, no antidote.

What can be done about AIDS?

While research scientists and physicians are charged with the primary responsibility for finding the means of preventing the disease and for curing those who have it, public concern must drive and support such an effort. That task rests with all of us.

There is, however, yet another, more personal task. I feel each of us must demonstrate compassion for those who have the virus and give loving care to those whose minds and bodies have been ravaged by the opportunistic diseases that accompany AIDS and inevitably lead to death.

Above all, do not push away your children or your siblings who reveal that they are gay. Recognize that for them this is as natural and as incurable as being left-handed. They, too, are at risk of becoming infected with the virus. To deprive them of your love and support when they so desperately need it will inevitably create festering resentment and despair for you and for them.

All who care for people with AIDS need our prayers, understanding, and help. AIDS strikes those we love the most: our sons, our brothers, our cousins, our friends, and our lovers. Now, sadly, even mothers and infants are stricken. Because we love them, we become their primary caretakers, but the process of caring for them—knowing of their inevitable demise—saps our strength, wrenches our emotions, and tests our faith.

~

It was our friend Monsignor Robert Wister who drew my attention to a newspaper clipping reproducing the memorial card of Joe McGarry, who died in Glasgow, Scotland, the day after Christmas in 1993. It is reprinted here with the kind permission of his daughter, Colette Sherry. The card expresses best the passage from life to death and gives comfort to those who have lost someone dear to them.

> Death is nothing at all. I have only slipped away into the next room. I am I, and you are you. Whatever we were to each other, that we still are. Call me by my old familiar name, speak to me in the easy way you always used. Put no difference into your tone, wear no forced air of solemnity or sorrow. Laugh as we always laughed at the little jokes we enjoyed together. Play, smile, think of me. Pray for me. Let my name be the household name it always was. Let it be spoken without the shadow of a ghost in it. Life means all that it ever meant. It is the same as it ever was. What is death but a negligible accident? Why should I be out of your mind because I am out of your sight? All is well, nothing is lost. One brief moment and all will be as it was before.

Postscript

Seven months after Sean died, I wrote one more letter to President Bush to inform him that we had lost our son to AIDS. My letter to him and his poignant reply are worth recording here.

The Honorable George Bush
President of the United States
The White House
Washington, D.C. 20501

June 11, 1991

Dear President Bush:

A personal tragedy prevented me from maintaining my personal contact with you, although you have been much in my thoughts as you coped so effectively with one international crisis after another.

The tragedy is that our son, Sean, died of AIDS last October 6th after a long and debilitating illness. He was only 26 years old and was on the threshold of a brilliant career in international affairs when he was stricken.

Doctors did all they could, given their limited knowledge and resources at the time, but his death was inevitable as he lost one faculty after another and wasted away.

Perhaps the knowledge that your friend and former CIA associate lost his only child to this terrible plague will bring home to you the fact every family in America will soon suffer a similar loss. Sean was one of 100,000 people who have died of AIDS. But a million Americans are infected with the HIV virus and tens of thousands more are infected every year. They will all surely die prematurely unless someone quickly discovers a way to regenerate the T4 cells that fight off infection.

Surely nothing in America has a higher priority.

I am enclosing a *New York Times* article by Dr. Michael Gottlieb, who discovered the first case of AIDS 10 years ago. He makes some valid points and I want to make sure that you have read it. Most important now, I think, would be public assurance from you that the elimination of AIDS is your top domestic priority, and that you personally get this message across to those members of Congress capable of passing whatever legislation is necessary.

With best personal good wishes from Brenda and from me.

Respectfully,

Robert Hopkins
2226 48th Street, N.W.
Washington, D.C. 20007

THE WHITE HOUSE

WASHINGTON

July 22, 1991

Dear Robert:

Barbara and I were deeply saddened to learn
of the loss of your son. As parents, we understand the depth of your grief, which words can
never adequately describe. Rest assured that
my Administration is committed to the search
for a cure for this devastating disease.
Surely God has welcomed Sean into His loving
arms. May He also strengthen and console you
and Brenda. Barbara and I are keeping you in
our prayers. God bless you.

Sincerely,

G Bush

Mr. Robert Hopkins
2226 48th Street, N.W.
Washington, D.C. 20007

In memory of Sean P. Hopkins

1964-1990

Appendix A
When a Friend Has AIDS

- Don't avoid your friend. Be there. It gives hope. Be the friend, the loved one you've always been, especially now when it is most important.
- Touch your friend. A simple squeeze of the hand or a hug can let him or her know you still care. (Don't be afraid. AIDS cannot be contracted by touching or casual contact.)
- Call before you visit. Your friend may not feel up to a visitor that day. Don't be afraid to phone again and visit on another occasion.
- Weep and laugh with your friend. Don't be afraid to share such intimate experiences—they may enrich you both.
- Tell your friend what you'd like to do to help. If he or she agrees, do this. Keep any promises you make.
- Call to say you are bringing your friend's favorite food. But ask to make sure it is something he or she is able to eat. Be precise about the time you are coming. Bring the food in disposable containers, so your friend won't have to worry about washing dishes. Spend time sharing a meal.
- Be creative. Bring books, magazines, taped music, a wall poster, or home-baked cookies. All of these become important now and can bring warmth and joy.
- Bring along another friend who hasn't visited before.
- Volunteer to take your friend for a walk or an outing, but ask about and respect any limitations.
- If your friend is a parent, ask about and offer to help care for any children. Offer to bring them to visit if they are not living with your friend.
- Offer to help answer any letters or phone calls your friend may have difficulty dealing with.
- Offer to do household chores, perhaps by taking out the laundry, washing dishes, watering plants, feeding and walking pets. This may be appreciated more than you realize. But don't take away chores that your friend can still do. He or she has already lost enough. Ask before doing anything.

- Don't feel that you both always have to talk. It's OK to sit together reading, listening to music, watching television. Much can be expressed without words.
- Appointments with Social Security or Medicaid can often be frustrating and exhausting. Offer to accompany your friend to help fill out the forms. Stay with him or her until the business is finished.
- If your friend is a recovering alcoholic or drug user and is unable to get to his or her 12-step meeting, such as Alcoholics Anonymous, offer to call other people in the program to suggest they consider coming to his or her hospital room or home to hold a meeting.
- If your friend expresses concern about his or her looks, be gentle, but acknowledge these feelings. Just your listening may be all that is needed. Try pointing out some positive physical traits. It may make him or her feel better.
- Be prepared for your friend to get angry with you for no obvious reason, although you have been there and done everything you could. Permit this, but don't take it in a personal way. Remember, when a person is very ill, anger and frustration are often taken out on the people most loved because it's safe and will be understood.
- If you and your friend are religious, ask if you could pray or attend services together. Don't hesitate to share your faith with your friend. Spirituality can be very important at this time.
- Don't lecture or become angry with your friend if he or she seems to be handling the illness in a way that you think is inappropriate. Your friend may not be where you expect or need him or her to be.
- Check in with the people who are taking care of your friend. They too may be suffering. They need a break from the illness from time to time. Offer to stay with the person with AIDS in order to give the loved ones some free time. Invite them out or offer to accompany them places. Remember, they need someone to talk with as well.
- Finally, take care of yourself! Recognize your own feelings and respect them. Share your grief, your anger, your helplessness— whatever emotions you may have—either with friends and loved ones or in a support group. Getting the support you need during this crisis will help you to be really there for your friend.

Appendix B
Support Organizations

National Association of People With AIDS
Box 34056
Washington, DC 20043

National Catholic AIDS Network (NCAN)
PO Box 422-984
San Francisco, CA 94142-2984

AIDS Interfaith Network
300 I Street, NE, Suite 400
Washington, DC 20002

National Funeral Directors Association
1121 West Oklahoma
Milwaukee, WI 53227

The NAMES Project
AIDS Memorial Quilt
Box 14573
San Francisco, CA 94114

Mothers of AIDS Patients
c/o 3043 E Street
San Diego, CA 92102

American Red Cross
Office of HIV/AIDS Education
Local Chapter

About the Author

Robert Hopkins has had a varied career during his professional life: a combat cameraman for the U.S. Army in Europe during World War II; a screenwriter at 20th Century Fox Films; a producer of *Justice for All*, a documentary radio program in Hollywood; a radio producer with the Marshall Plan in Paris, documenting the accomplishments of this vast economic program, in close association with Averell Harriman; author of a Fodor's guidebook on France; a CIA covert agent in Europe and South America. Following his retirement from government service in 1980, he worked for several years as a political consultant for Transnational Executive Service. He is currently president of the Harry Hopkins Public Service Institute (named in honor of his father), a nonprofit corporation designed to encourage young people to embark on careers in public service and to recognize and reward outstanding public servants.

Hopkins lives with his wife, Brenda, in Washington, D.C., where they are active in various outreach efforts on behalf of HIV/AIDS victims in both the civic and religious arenas. Their son and only child succumbed to AIDS in 1990.